GUY DE LA BÉDOYÈRE

D0275800

ARCHITECTURE IN ROMAN BRITAIN

WITHDRA

SHIRE ARCHAEOLOGY

722.709362

Cover illustrations:
(Left) Part of the baths exercise hall at Leicester.
(Top right) The north gate at Housesteads fort, Hadrian's Wall.
(Bottom right) The fourth-century villa at Littlecote.
(Photographs and painting by the author)

1845

British Library Cataloguing in Publication Data:
De la Bédoyère, Guy
Architecture in Roman Britain. – (Shire archaeology; 81)
1. Architecture, Roman – Great Britain
I. Title
722.7'09361
ISBN 0 7478 0530 X

Published in 2002 by
SHIRE PUBLICATIONS LTD
Cromwell House, Church Street, Princes Risborough,
Buckinghamshire HP27 9AA, UK.
(Website: www.shirebooks.co.uk)

Series Editor: James Dyer.

Copyright © Guy de la Bédoyère 2002.

Guy de la Bédoyère is hereby identified as the author of this work in accordance with Section 77 of the Copyright, Designs and Patents Act, 1988.

All rights reserved.
No part of this publication may be reproduced or transmitted in any form or by any means, electronic or mechanical, including photocopy, recording, or any information storage and retrieval system, without permission in writing from the publishers.

Number 81 in the Shire Archaeology series.

ISBN 0 7478 0530 X.

First published 2002.

Printed in Great Britain by
CIT Printing Services Ltd, Press Buildings,
Merlins Bridge, Haverfordwest, Pembrokeshire SA61 1XF.

Contents

List of illustrations

Foreword and acknowledgements

Roman buildings in Britain often seem disappointing lumps of masonry and tile. Britain's weather and dynamic history have led to most of these remarkable structures being demolished, burned down or buried. It is hard to believe that all these were once forts, public buildings, homes and defences. No building of the Roman period stands intact in Britain, and we cannot link any known architect to a single one.

But archaeology, and comparisons with buildings elsewhere in the Roman world, make it possible to understand how these places once appeared, and what they were like to live and work in. Britain was home to some impressive examples of architecture. This book is about bringing back to life some of these remarkable buildings, and helping the reader to see and take pleasure in Roman Britain as a world of three dimensions. It concentrates on particular examples drawn from different aspects of life in Roman Britain in order to show what sort of designs, decorations and techniques were involved in the first great period of architecture in Britain. These range from the masonry bulwarks of the military granaries at Housesteads to the elegant Orphic hall at Littlecote. There is no doubt that some of these buildings were amongst the most impressive that Britain has ever seen and they deserve to be remembered.

I would like to thank Bill Griffiths at Wallsend and James Dyer for their help with the text. All photographs, drawings and paintings are by myself unless otherwise mentioned.

Guy de la Bédoyère, Welby 2002

Glossary

Ambulatory: covered passageway.
Anaerobic: conditions in which lack of oxygen prevents decomposition of organic items.
Apse: semicircular chamber protruding from a room.
Architrave: carved block that is part of the frame to a door or window, or that spans columns.
Ashlar: blocks of dressed stone (cut to regular shapes with smoothed faces).
Balustrade: low wall on the side of a roof or balcony.
Basilica: hall consisting of nave and aisles (figures 4, 29).
Bastion: projecting tower installed on city or fort walls.
Buttress: a wall support.
Caldarium: hot chamber in a bath suite.
Cella: inner chamber of a temple, where the god's likeness was displayed.
Centurial stone: stone inscribed by a military century (see *century*), recording its building work (see figure 18).
Century: unit of eighty soldiers, made up of ten tent-parties of eight men (see figure 18).
Finial: decorative roof terminal, set at the apex, sometimes as a carved stone chimney.
Frigidarium: cold chamber in a bath suite.
Groma: a mitre or set square, usually made of bronze, used by architects and surveyors (see figure 8).
Hypocaust: pipes and voids under floors and through walls carrying air heated by a furnace.
Imbrices: curved roof tiles laid over the joints between *tegulae.*
Insulae: blocks in towns marked out by a street-grid.
Mensor: surveyor.
Municipium: category of Roman town with Latin citizen status.
Narthex: area between the entrance of a church and the beginning of the aisles and nave.
Norma: a mitre or set square, used for laying out angles on a building (see figure 8).
Overshot: mill wheel turned by water flowing from over the top. See also *undershot.*
Pedes Monetales: Roman units of measurement equivalent to 2.21 metres (7 feet 3 inches).
Pediment: triangular top part of a temple façade, usually containing decorative sculptures.
Pes: Roman foot measure, equivalent to 29.6 cm (11.5 inches).

Pilae: piers made of square tiles in stacks, supporting a raised floor so that hot air in a *hypocaust* system can circulate freely.

Putlog holes: recesses left in masonry walls where wooden scaffolding poles were secured (see cover, and figures 13, 31).

Structura caementicia: cemented rubble core packed inside two facing walls of dressed stone and brick.

Tegulae: large square roof tiles with flanged edges to left and right.

Temenos: the sacred enclosure surrounding a temple, its altar and associated monuments.

Tepidarium: warm chamber in a bath suite.

Tetrastyle: temple façade made of four columns supporting a *pediment*.

Tholos: circular temple with an outer colonnade, based on Greek design.

Triconch: three apses arranged in the form of a cross.

Undershot: mill wheel turned by water flowing underneath. See also *overshot*.

Wattle and daub: timber frame, interlaced with twigs (wattles), packed with mud and straw (daub).

The north gate of the colony at Lincoln is the only Roman gate in Britain that traffic still passes through. Originally the single-portal entrance to the city was flanked by pedestrian passages on both sides. Early third century.

1
The coming of architecture

Before the Romans arrived in AD 43, there was no architecture in Britain as we understand it. For all the complexity of prehistoric monuments, such as stone circles, and chambered tombs built of stone slabs, permanent stone buildings did not form part of everyday life.

By the late Iron Age, some British tribes were producing sophisticated structures to defend and control their territory, and to live in. Hillforts, intimidating expressions of power, involved colossal amounts of skilled labour to create the ditches, mounds and fortified gateways (figure 1). Roundhouses, built from timber, wattle and daub, were waterproof and warm homes, which could last for many years, and some circular temples were being built.

The arrival of the Roman army also meant the coming of professional architects to Britain. Mostly of military origin, they laid out forts and supervised troops in building a range of structures literally inconceivable to the local inhabitants (figure 2). Symmetrical and regular, the buildings belonged to a complex system linking them into the rest of the ancient

1. The late Iron Age hillfort at Maiden Castle (Dorset), looking west along the south-facing ramparts. Hillforts represented the pinnacle of pre-Roman military architecture in Britain. But they proved hopelessly obsolete when confronted by the Roman army in AD 43 and afterwards.

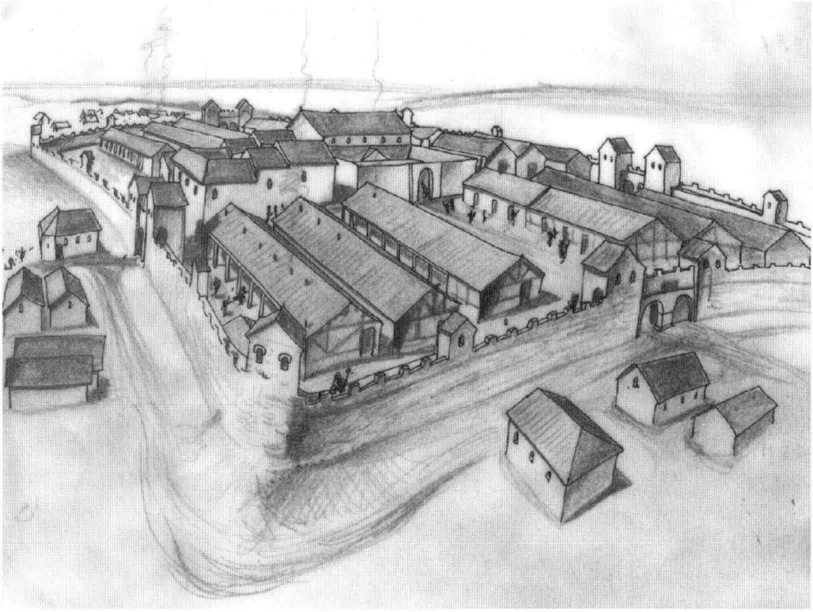

2. Drawing of a Roman fort, similar to those along Hadrian's Wall. Monumental gateways and defences surround the compound in which barracks and granaries cluster around the commandant's house and the headquarters building. These miniature military towns featured a huge range of building styles and techniques.

world, alongside provision for water supply, ventilation, drainage and roads.

The Roman historian Josephus was fascinated by how the Roman army would set up for an overnight stop, likening the result to a 'boom town with a market, workers' huts, and places for officers of all ranks to sort out arguments' (*Jewish War* iii.4). The remains of forts in Britain testify to the provision of barracks, stables, granaries and baths.

Roman architecture is one of antiquity's greatest legacies, though Britain's Roman buildings pale into insignificance compared with the monuments of Italy, North Africa and the Near East. However, excavations have shown that Britain was home to building on a grand scale, including some very imaginative experiments in classical architecture. Roman power and government used building as potent expressions of authority, which British and American architects of the eighteenth and nineteenth centuries recognised and emulated.

Cities were at the heart of Roman administration and commerce. From them regions were governed, and populations integrated into Roman life. Public buildings were essential, and their provision was

3. The façade of the temple of Claudius at Colchester. Built in the mid first century AD, the temple was destroyed by Boudican rebels in 60/61 and was rebuilt. Today it survives only as foundations and vaults under the Norman castle, but the proportions allow it to be reconstructed on paper according to the canons of classical architecture.

needed to attract town dwellers. But in the Eastern Empire, the Roman conquerors took advantage of the great cities like Ephesus and Alexandria. In Britain, there was nothing like them. Urban-style settlements, typically the late Iron Age *oppida*, mainly in the south-east, were diffuse areas defined by dykes and natural barriers like rivers and containing scattered traces of occupation.

Romano-British towns were first created by settling retired Roman legionaries in colonies specifically founded as examples of the benefits of Roman town life and as a trained reserve for emergencies. Other towns were established near tribal settlements, often, like Cirencester, on the site of a former fort. They benefited from the roads established to supply the former fort but probably also received government money and manpower for public buildings. London, conversely, grew up around the bridge over the Thames purely as a result of the effects of commerce.

Reporting on the Boudican Revolt in the year 60/61, Tacitus tells us that the new colony at Colchester was already equipped with a theatre, senate house and temple (*Annals* xiv.32). This was only seventeen years after the Roman invasion (figure 3). Although Colchester, London and St Albans were wiped out in the Revolt, new towns had sprung from the ashes within a generation (figure 29). By the second century, most major towns had public buildings. The reaction of the Romano-British can only be imagined, but the first experience of entering a basilican government hall must have been overwhelming (figure 4).

Architecture took longer to impact on the more general population's everyday life but many rural homes underwent a transition from roundhouse to rectangular house within fifty years of the Roman invasion. Throughout Romano-British society the preference for Roman-type structures was constantly repeated, finding its greatest expression in the great fourth-century villas (figure 46). But everyone could benefit from facilities as diverse as theatres, bridges and lighthouses.

Religious building seems to have been especially popular in Roman Britain. More temples are recorded on inscriptions than any other class of building. Temples were also some of the most intriguing types of structure, including the astonishing 'Arthur's O'on', which survived as late as the mid eighteenth century before being demolished (figure 5). Architectural motifs also appeared on wall paintings and carved reliefs, including tombstones (figure 6).

4. The interior of a Romano-British basilican government hall would have been almost indistinguishable from this view of the interior of the church of Santa Sabina, built *c.*425 in Rome. Here the apse contains an altar, but the government basilica had a raised tribunal from where officials could address public assemblies and dispense justice. The basilica provided the perfect model for Christian churches, which have thereby preserved the design.

5. The stone 'beehive' structure, apparently a temple, known as 'Arthur's O'on' or 'Oven', built close to Carron near the Antonine Wall in Scotland. Built *c.*130–60, destroyed in 1743. From an old engraving.

6. Tombstones and reliefs.
(Left) The tombstone of Regina, the British freedwoman and wife of Barates from Palmyra in Syria, from South Shields. The tombstone has an architectural frame with pediment and floral columns recalling buildings found in the Eastern Empire. Early third century. From an old engraving.
(Right) Relief from a temple of Jupiter Dolichenus at Corbridge (Northumberland) depicting Castor or Pollux awaiting the sun-god beneath a pair of columns under a decorative pediment. Third century.

Some ambitious buildings defy easy classification. At Stonea Grange (Cambridgeshire) a settlement grew up in the early second century. The centrepiece seems to have been a monumental tower in the middle of a piazza. It has been suggested that the tower formed a landmark administrative centre for an imperial estate and was perhaps intended to attract urban growth. In the middle of the flat Fens it would have been very imposing, but the settlement never grew and by *c.*200 the tower had been demolished. At Castor, near Peterborough, a vast winged building that resembled an eighteenth-century Palladian stately home looked across the Fenland from a hill. It also might have been the headquarters of an imperial estate. But the truth is that both buildings remain mysteries.

The process of building is something of a mystery. We know very little about the architects – and apart from some military examples, we do not even know their names. Despite their imagination and industry, some made significant mistakes. The designer of the temple of Apollo at Nettleton omitted to include buttresses and it collapsed (figure 41). Other architects ignored local conditions, such as the consequences of building over filled-in ditches. As a result the basilica at Cirencester and the hall at Littlecote suffered subsidence (figure 42).

Public building on any scale had dwindled by the third century but architectural skills were kept alive by contemporary bouts of fort building and restoration, followed by the great villa-building boom of the fourth century. By about 375, even that had ceased. With very few exceptions, villa houses seem to have been left to crumble into oblivion. In fifth-century Wroxeter people lived and traded amongst the ruins of old public buildings. Careful excavation here has shown that building in timber, notoriously difficult to detect at any time, became pre-eminent once more. It is impossible to know how much building and town life continued, particularly as coinage and pottery had largely gone out of use, leaving archaeologists little with which to track and date occupation. Either way, it is clear that Roman architecture had dwindled as quickly as it had once appeared.

2
Techniques and materials

Around the end of the second century, Amandus, *arc(h)itectus*, literally 'engineer', commissioned a carving of the goddess Brigantia (a deity representing the tribal area in northern England) and dedicated it at the fort of Birrens, *Blatobulgium*, a few miles north-west of Hadrian's Wall (figure 7). Although Amandus is not the only Roman architect known from Roman Britain, all those who are have turned up in the military zone.

One of the best-known surviving Roman books is *On Architecture* by Marcus Vitruvius Pollio, written in the late first century BC. Vitruvius believed an architect should master history, drawing, geometry, music (for acoustics) and even medicine so that he could assess a site's susceptibility to disease or pestilence. Most of all, an architect needed to understand theory as well as practice, and to be able to write all this down to leave a record of his work for future generations.

Amandus needed to know everything about the techniques available to him, and where to find the materials required to build anything from a timber-laced earthen rampart to a fully plumbed and ventilated fort bath-house (figure 8).

Military architects were probably used to help in urban building. Elsewhere in the Empire, soldiers played vital roles in civilian building projects. In the mid second century, Nonius Datus, veteran surveyor of the Third Legion Augusta, based in Africa, was called out of retirement to help the town of Saldae in the

7. Carved relief depicting Brigantia, the personification of the spirit of what is now northern England. Dedicated by Amandus the *arc(h)itectus* ('engineer'). Found at the fort of Birrens (Dumfries and Galloway).

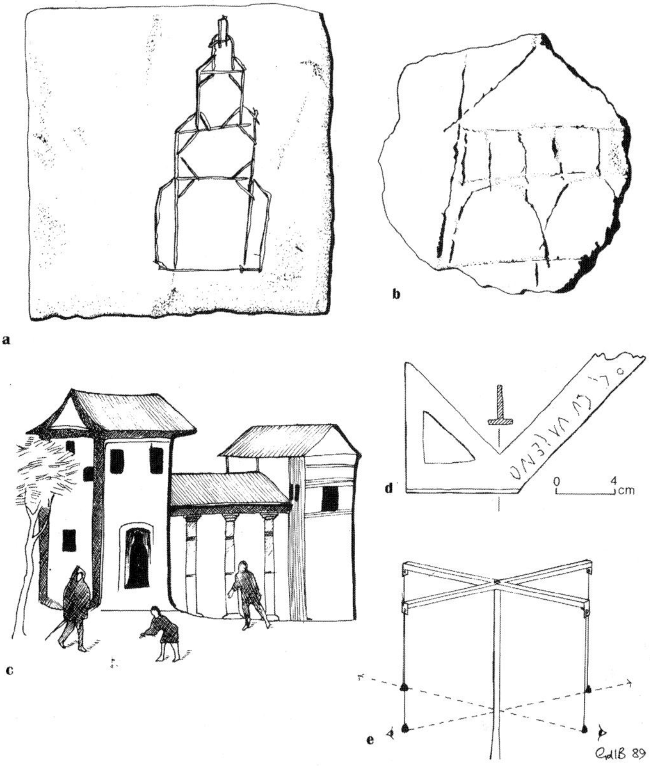

8. Equipment and designs. (a) A tile from London depicting what may be a building design. (b) A scratched drawing on wall plaster from the house at Hucclecote (Gloucestershire), apparently showing a villa façade. (c) A drawing of a house shown on wall plaster found at Trier (Germany) with towers and a colonnaded portico. (d) A bronze *norma* (set square), used for laying out right-angles, found in Canterbury (Kent). (e) A *groma*, used for setting out the sides of buildings, and streets.

province of Mauretania Caesariensis. The townsfolk were digging out a tunnel through a mountain to supply water to their city. They had started on opposite sides of the mountain and the two parties had failed to meet up. Nonius had to sort things out. We only know this because he was mugged *en route* to the job, recording the adventure later on an inscription. Later on, the emperor Probus (276–82) was said to have ordered his soldiers to build public works in Egyptian cities.

Nonius shows that, in a place that had been a province just a little longer than Britain, still only a retired legionary surveyor was skilled enough to complete a major project. In Britain, where soldiers dominate

9. The theatre at St Albans looking south across the north entrance. The banks supported wooden seats and were revetted by the buttressed flint-and-tile walls in the foreground. One of the stage's four columns survives. The figures in the background are walking along Watling Street, which ran through the centre of the town, in the direction of the basilica–forum complex that lay under the trees at upper right.

the record and where there was no tradition of architecture, military surveyors and architects must have been detailed to lay out towns and design some public buildings in order to kick-start the process. The governor Agricola (*c.*78–84) is said to have encouraged individuals and communities to build temples, forums and houses (Tacitus, *Agricola* 21). He probably utilised soldiers to help with the work.

Surveyors and architects

Amandus worked alongside men like Attonius Quintianus, *mensor*, 'surveyor'. Attonius is recorded on an inscription from Piercebridge fort (Durham). Surveyors used the *groma* and a *norma* to lay out the street-grid of a fort or a town and then allocated zones for individual buildings (figure 8). The late-Roman military writer Vegetius describes how surveyors measured out the ground for each block of ten men (*On Military Affairs* iii.8). Surveyors used standard units of measurement called *pedes Monetales*, or the standard Roman foot (*pes*). Sometimes it is possible to detect their use by careful measurement of excavated sites, particularly where the original surveyors used a regular pattern of multiples of the basic unit. For example, the fortress at Colchester was laid out with 200 foot and 300 foot wide strips.

This sounds inflexible but actual fort layouts show that local conditions and contours were taken into account. So, no two forts are the same and once land was set aside for a specific building it was not necessarily erected there immediately, or built to the size allowed for. At the short-lived turf-and-timber legionary fortress of Inchtuthil (*c.*83–7), land was set aside for the headquarters building and the commandant's house. The latter was never built and the headquarters, as executed, was much smaller than the space provided and clearly temporary.

The major towns of Roman Britain almost all had street-grids laid out based on square or rectangular *insulae*. That planning for a full suite of public buildings was involved is plain from St Albans. Here a prime site near the forum was set aside. The plot remained vacant for many years until the theatre was built and must have been designated for it from the outset (figure 9). At Silchester (Hampshire), the orientation of buildings shows that at least two phases of surveying took place, the second at a slightly different angle.

Where the chosen site had problems, Roman engineers were often able to correct them. Fishbourne 'palace' was substantially enlarged and rebuilt as early as the 70s AD. The new building was so big that the sloping land would have affected its appearance. Soil and fill were dug

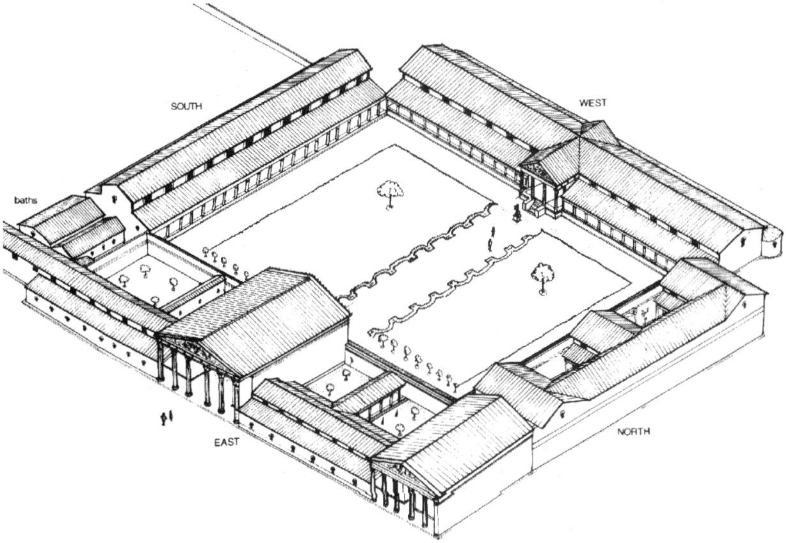

10. Fishbourne palace, near Chichester (West Sussex) as it might have appeared in the late first century. The house was unprecedented in Britain for the period and was not matched by any other for two centuries. Its size and decoration mean that it must have been built either for a Roman official, perhaps the governor, or a pro-Roman client king. It was destroyed by fire at the end of the third century.

out of the western, higher side and packed on to the eastern, lower side until a much more level site had been created (figure 10).

There is no Romano-British building we can tie to the name of its architect. Building inscriptions tend to record the name of the emperor, the governor of the province and either the military unit or civic organisation responsible. Many Roman buildings conform to basic stereotypes. The forum and basilica in the western provinces, for example, are very similar to the military headquarters building. This suggests that the urban architects knew the military version well (or vice-versa), and perhaps the same men were responsible, and probably worked from textbooks of standard measurements and layouts to prepare plans. One of the few examples of a possible 'on-site' sketch turned up on a tile from London. It has been identified as a representation of a lighthouse but might also be a section through a more complex structure – perhaps a basilica (figure 8).

The exceptional 'Elliptical Building' in the legionary fortress at Chester (*Deva*) is evidence that some plans must have been prepared and stored (figure 12). This unparalleled building's function is unknown but it meant the whole fortress footprint, laid out in the late first century, was specially designed to accommodate it. Curiously, it was just set out and begun before being abandoned and buried. More than a century later, legionary architects set to work once more and erected a very similar building at a higher level over the fill covering the early version. The

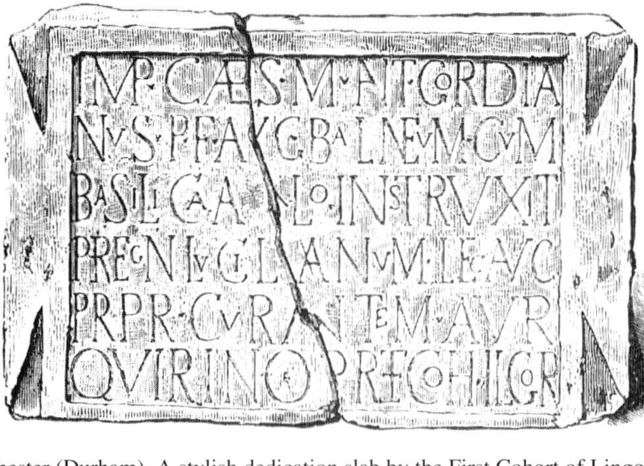

11. Lanchester (Durham). A stylish dedication slab by the First Cohort of Lingonians in the reign of Gordian III (238–44), recording the erection of a bath with basilica under the governorship of Egnatius Lucilianus. Inscriptions like this are important evidence for buildings that have not yet been located or excavated. *Balneum* for baths appears in line 2, and *Basilica* in line 3.

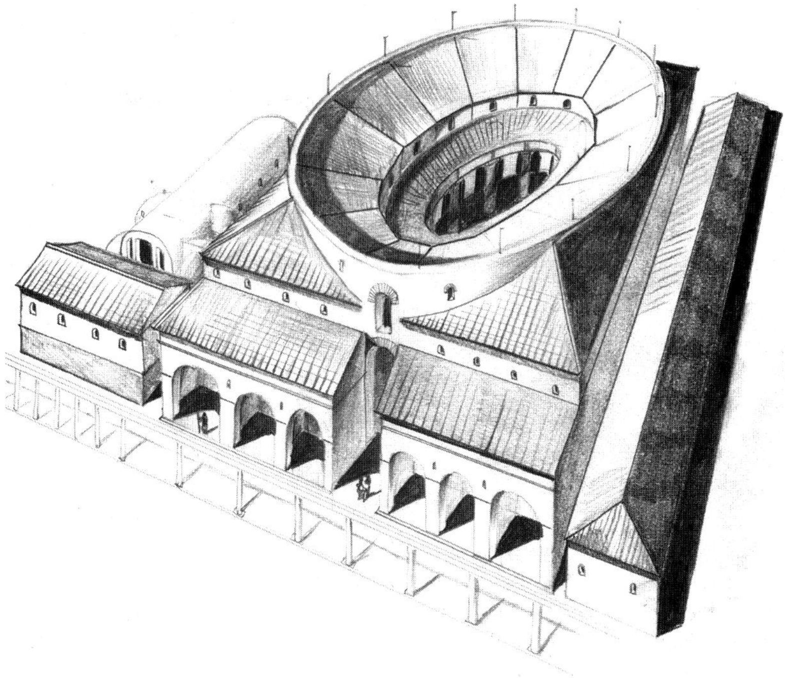

12. The 'Elliptical Building' at the legionary fortress of Chester (Cheshire), as it might have appeared had it been completed to the late-first-century design. More than a century later a similar building was erected on the site but the purpose of either remains a mystery. Nothing else like it is known.

third-century architects must have had access to plans, stored in the fortress archives, prepared by their long-dead predecessors.

There are many inscriptions from the third century in Britain that record restoration of military buildings, especially on the northern frontier. As most were around a century old by then, natural decay was probably responsible. Sometimes projects had gathered dust. At Netherby fort, near Hadrian's Wall, a cavalry exercise hall 'long ago begun from the ground' (so says the inscription) was finally completed under Severus Alexander in 222.

However, in the early second century Pliny the Younger was governor of Bithynia and Pontus in Asia Minor (north-west Turkey). He wrote frequently to the Emperor Trajan (98–117) to tell him about disastrous civic building projects. Nicomedia, for instance, started two expensive aqueduct projects that were abandoned due to incompetence. Pliny wanted Trajan to send an architect to sort the mess out (*Letters* x.37). At Nicaea, a theatre costing 10 million sesterces (a legion's pay for nearly two years) started to subside into ill-prepared ground (*ibid.* x.39).

If great cities in the East could suffer from incompetent builders, then it is hardly surprising that some fort buildings in northern Britain could fall down or urban forums subside. This makes it hard for an archaeologist to be sure a stone wall is thick enough to have carried an upper storey as an incompetent architect could easily have installed one on walls not strong enough to bear it. Several Romano-British buildings have now given up details of their façades, for instance the houses at Redlands Farm (Stanwick) and Meonstoke (figures 45, 51, 52). Badly prepared foundations or other problems caused sections of wall to fall over, preserving the original form of the buildings.

Some buildings were not completed. The cross-hall of the Second Legion Augusta's fortress at Caerleon seems to have been unfinished, and London's great Hadrianic basilica – which would have been the biggest Roman structure north of the Alps – may also have been abandoned during construction. The 'bridge' at Piercebridge has defied conclusive interpretation. Perhaps it too was left incomplete, leaving confusing remains.

Timber

Surviving traces of Roman buildings are almost always stone, brick or concrete. But timber (*materia*) played a vital part in Romano-British building. It was easily available and flexible because it could be dismantled and reused. During the first century AD most military buildings, and even some public buildings, were made of wood, putting pressure on stocks of seasoned timber. The wharf-builders at London became increasingly dependent on freshly felled timber, which rots more quickly (figure 54). This may have encouraged the move to stone for other public and military buildings.

Timber structures can normally be identified only when archaeologists find traces of post-holes or wall trenches dug for horizontal beams. Fire can carbonise timber, and sometimes traces of burnt wood remain visible.

Vertical timbers were either placed in the post-holes or secured to the horizontal beams. Around these a frame was built, packed with wattle and daub, and held together with iron nails or wooden pegs. Sometimes, a timber frame was filled with brick. Vitruvius was not enthusiastic about wattle and daub, believing it to be poor quality, inflammable and unstable (ii.8.20). This is demonstrated by the burnt layers in London, Colchester and St Albans from the Boudican Revolt, preserving traces of these early shops and houses destroyed by fire.

During the second century, town and country houses were increasingly built in stone, though many houses may have had stone footings but timber superstructures. Since none of these houses survives much above its foundations, it is very hard to tell in any one case.

Wood continued to be important, as it does today, for roofing and flooring. But timber's greatest enemy, apart from fire, is damp. Timbers inserted into the ground were bound to decay within a generation, and moisture from hot baths made wooden roofs unsuitable. As Roman Britain became more settled, timber began to give way to other materials where durability and size were paramount.

Stone, concrete and brick

The resistance of these materials to fire makes them extremely useful, but they were also essential for creating impressive structures like public buildings, bath-houses and monumental arches. In northern and western Britain, building stone is more widely available, explaining why so many frontier forts, and those in Wales, remain impressive monuments.

Stone buildings depended on good foundations. A trench was dug and filled with rubble courses set in mortar. On soft and wet land, a timber raft was created first by driving timber piles deep down into the subsoil. This was particularly suitable for supporting bridge piers but is also found underneath some fort or urban defences.

Masonry construction required much effort to quarry and transport the blocks, and skill to dress and assemble them. A gate needed arch stones, sill stones with pivot-holes for doors, chamfered stones for levelling courses, as well as blocks carved with hemispherical cut-outs so that they could act as window arches (figure 19 and page 7). More decorative buildings might also need features such as classical columns and architraves.

In south-east Britain, builders were more dependent on material like ragstone. These irregular lumps of flint had to be carefully shaped, assembled into walls and secured with mortar. Tile courses, placed at regular horizontal intervals and at corners, served much as a timber frame would have done and helped stabilise the structure. In the Saxon period and later, this tile was often extracted for reuse, leaving characteristic voids in Roman city walls, for example at St Albans.

A mortared rubble core could reduce the amount of dressed stone needed and speed the building process, even if it was less durable. This was the miracle of Roman building, called by the Romans *opus caementicium*, and by us 'Roman concrete'. Walls could be faced with tile or stone, but the mortar core gave it strength and allowed large and complex buildings to be erected quickly.

By varying the rubble ('aggregate') according to requirements, this simple concrete could be the basis of massive walls or vaults and is found widely in Britain. In its most advanced form, Roman concrete was good enough to be the sole material used in a vault and was created by pouring concrete into wooden moulds.

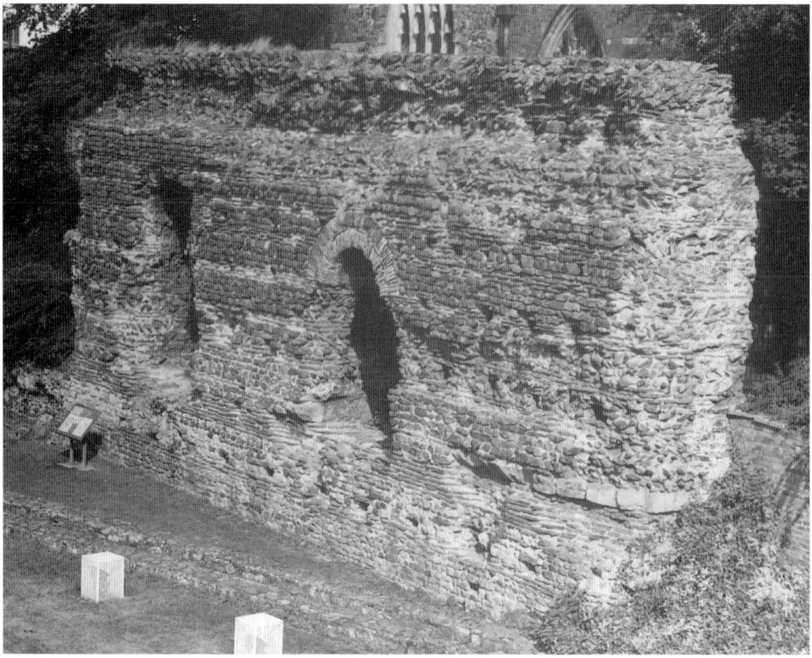

13. The Jewry Wall at Leicester (see also front cover). This masonry formed part of the baths' exercise hall and probably owes its preservation to being incorporated into an early medieval church. The arches allowed access between the hall and the baths. The tile courses are visible, as are the putlog holes.

Walls with concrete cores were not entirely secure. Vitruvius warned that any damage to the facing could allow water in (i.8.8). The water loosened the core and, if it froze, caused the mortar to break up. This is why Hadrian's Wall was rebuilt on many occasions. Today, it still needs regular remedial work.

Roofing

Made of fired clay, or cut from stone, roof tiles are found in huge numbers on Roman sites (figure 45). The basic units were the *tegulae* and the *imbrices*. Brittle and heavy (a *tegula* could weigh 5.4 kg or 12 pounds), they needed substantial support from stout roof timbers. When those rotted they collapsed to the floor and around the building, shattering into innumerable fragments. Not all the tiles needed to be nailed to the timbers – the weight alone was enough – but many do have nail holes, even more necessary on limestone roof tiles. See *Pottery in Roman Britain* (pp. 61–2) in the Shire Archaeology series for more details.

Ceramic roof tiles were manufactured close to the building site if the basic raw materials were available. The same process produced flat tiles used for levelling courses, flooring or hypocaust *pilae*, and the hollow box flue-tiles, which piped warm air through walls.

Barrel (semicircular) vaults were ideal for roofing bath-houses. By not using timber, rot was prevented and a fire risk avoided, but vaults were much heavier. The Great Bath at Bath seems to have been remodelled in the late second century to replace a rotten timber-and-tile roof with a barrel vault. The extra weight meant the supporting piers had to be substantially strengthened (figure 14).

Vaults were made as light as possible by using concrete made with tufa aggregate, with moulded recesses, and introducing ribs made of hollow ceramic or tufa tiles. Volcanic tufa was ideal because it is light and strong, but supplies had to be imported from Germany. The military bath-house at Chesters on Hadrian's Wall has produced many traces of its vaulted roof (figure 26).

14. Pier from the Great Bath at Bath (Somerset). The lateral forces created by a vault required colossal reinforcements to piers, often aided by buttresses. These can be seen here, added to either side of the original pier.

Decoration and comfort

Mosaic floors and painted wall plaster are dealt with by other books in the Shire Archaeology series (see 'Further reading') but, to sum up, they formed integral parts of some buildings such as the Orphic floor in the triple-apsed ('triconch') hall at Littlecote (see chapter 6 and figure 42). Exotic stone veneers were also used in some prestige buildings in Britain, but they generally survive only as fragments or splinters. Traces of stone imported from all over the Mediterranean have been found in Britain, for example at Canterbury, London, and even Woodchester villa.

Decorative architectural features such as columns and carved reliefs turn up more frequently but are rarely found *in situ* (figure 49). Major military buildings, public buildings and temples were frequently decorated with classical columns, floral wreaths, decorative architraves and sculptured images. One of the most important innovations brought by the Romans was glass in all its forms. Buildings frequently yield modest traces of the characteristically crude and opaque, almost translucent, green window glass used.

Dating buildings

The only certain way to date a building is if an inscription is found (figure 11). But these are scarce and are usually found reused as building blocks or in some other context. They are rarely found in the building to which they once belonged. Instead, conventional dating tools must be used. A building at Castleford (West Yorkshire) had an almost mint-condition coin of Vespasian (69–79) packed into a wattle-and-daub wall, which was therefore probably erected within ten to fifteen years of that date. More usually, archaeologists rely on coins and pottery found sealed in floor layers, ditches or rubbish pits associated with the structure.

3
Military defences

Earth and timber

During the first century AD, most fort defences in Roman Britain were built of earth-and-timber ramparts with timber gateways. As effective as stone, they were quickly erected by using turf and soil from defensive ditches for the ramparts. However, drying earth causes ramparts to sink under their own weight, and wet weather erodes them. Timber lacing was used as reinforcement by laying horizontal and vertical posts in the earth as ramparts were built up. Outer faces were strengthened

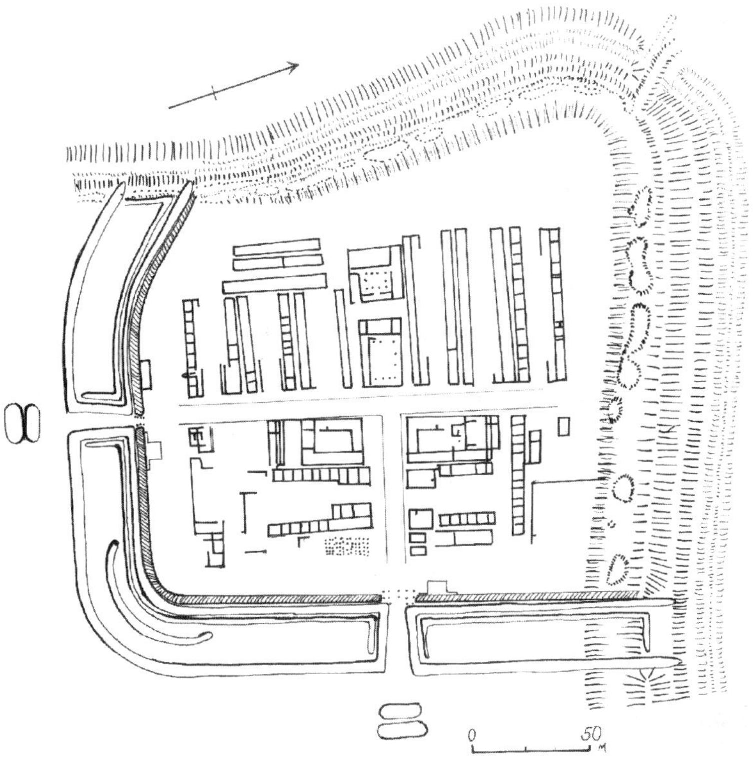

15. Plan of the Claudian turf-and-timber fort at Hod Hill (Dorset). The fort was built in a corner of the Iron Age hillfort, utilising some of the old defences in doing so. The hillfort was probably seized during the conquest in the mid 40s.

with turfs or timber planking. Along the top, more planks provided a walkway for soldiers, protected by a palisade of staves.

The technique was the most effective way of quickly establishing a durable military base, which could last for around a decade or more before needing major reconstruction. Hod Hill (Dorset) is one of the earliest known forts in Britain (figure 15). Here the army exploited an Iron Age hillfort's ditches to provide two sides of the Roman fort, showing that military surveyors were practical and flexible.

Timber gateways leave only post-holes, metal fittings and road surfacing for the archaeologist to identify. Typical remains are a pair of towers marked by four or six holes each and a gate, or two gates, in between (figure 16). Iron sheathing for gate pivots sometimes also survives. In the late first century, turf-and-timber forts still provided the backbone of the conquest of the north. The legionary fortress at Inchtuthil was built this way in *c.*83–7. The fortress was abandoned within five years, with the entire complex being dismantled and levelled, leaving little or no trace on the surface.

16. Reconstructed model of a timber gate of the type used in first-century forts, for example Longthorpe (Cambridgeshire). Functional and efficient, they were ideal for forts unlikely to be in use for more than ten or twenty years. Now on display at Peterborough Museum.

Stone defences

Stone defences belong to the military consolidation of the late first century, when permanent installations were established. These include the legionary fortresses at Caerleon (Second Legion Augusta), Chester (Twentieth Legion) and York (Ninth Legion, and after 122 the Sixth Legion). It was normal to adapt existing turf ramparts by shaving off the outside face and installing a stone facing. But even new forts usually had an earthen bank packed up behind the stone walls. None survives to full height in Britain, but a collapsed section of wall found at Wörth in Germany shows that the parapet walkway was about 4.5 metres (15 feet) above the ground. On top of this was a parapet of 1.6 metres (5 feet) in height with crenellations, resembling a medieval castle.

The frontier Walls

Hadrian's Wall was begun *c.*122–4 and resembles an unfolded fort wall stretching across Britain. There was nothing else exactly like it in the Roman Empire. By the time it was finished (if indeed it ever was), the Wall system consisted of a free-standing curtain wall about 3.5–4.5

17. Section of reconstructed Hadrian's Wall at Wallsend. The foundations of the original stretch, which suffered partial collapse, can be seen in the foreground. The height and appearance of the Wall are hypothetical.

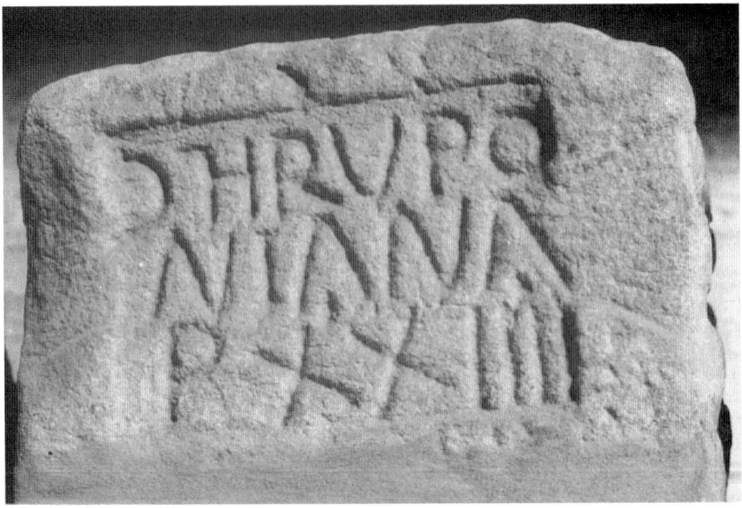

18. Centurial stone from the fort of Carrawburgh on Hadrian's Wall, recording that the Thruponian century had built '*p(edes) XXIIII*' ('24 feet worth [of rampart]'). About 130–40.

metres (11–15 feet) high, a small fortlet (called by us a 'milecastle') every mile, turrets at roughly one-third of a mile intervals between them, and a forward ditch. The system was soon modified by adding forts roughly every 10 km (6 miles), as well as a rearward ditch-and-mound system we call the 'Vallum'.

The Wall has been examined in minute detail and excavation has shown that the Roman builders changed the Wall's specifications almost from the outset. It was begun at a width of 10 Roman feet, but soon an 8 foot curtain was being built on completed sections of 10 foot foundation and joined up to completed milecastles prepared for a 10 foot curtain. The new forts, including Housesteads, were built by demolishing sections of Wall already built. To begin with, the entire western half was built of turf, with turf milecastles but stone turrets. By the middle of the second century this had all been replaced with stone. Clearly, the Wall's plans were modified 'in the field'. Later on, parts of the system, such as turrets and milecastle gates, were demolished or blocked, showing that the Wall was used differently at different times.

Hadrian's Wall has one of the best records of rampart building. The work was mostly done by centuries detached from each of the three legions. These centuries installed on the Wall, and sometimes in fort walls, inscribed 'centurial stones', which identified the centuries and how much they had built (figure 18). Possibly as a matter of pride, they also allowed inspectors to identify culprits responsible for bad building.

Parts of Hadrian's Wall seem to have been whitewashed. This would have made the frontier more imposing and also exposed sections needing repair.

All 59 km (37 Roman miles) of the short-lived Antonine Wall, built *c.*140–3 between the Forth and the Clyde, was made of turf and timber. This time a cobble base with a width of 14 Roman feet (4.1 metres) was laid down the whole way. However, turrets and vallum were omitted. Although the Antonine Wall was in use for little more than a generation, many traces remain visible today.

Gates

Fort gates were always the most imposing part of the defences. A gate had to provide accommodation for defenders, storage space, complete visibility of the route in and out of the fort, easy transport of goods, horses and men, while being able to be closed and secured at a moment's notice.

Today, there is no better example than the west gate at South Shields (figure 19). This gate has been completely rebuilt on the original foundations, using evidence from sites around the Roman frontier. Most fort gates on the northern frontier were probably similar, though it is unknown if the towers were roofed. Doors were made of reinforced timber. They swung on iron pivots slotted into holes cut into the stone.

19. Reconstructed west gate at South Shields. Built on original foundations and facsimiles of architectural features (like window-heads) found in the vicinity, this structure is a mixture of speculation and hard research.

20. The north gate of milecastle 37 on Hadrian's Wall as it might have appeared in the second century. On either side, small barracks accommodated the dozen or so troops who manned these fortified passageways through the Wall. Built by the Second Legion Augusta *c.*122–4.

Once installed, the pivot was secured with lead.

Gates were ideal places to display monumental inscriptions. Some featured carved reliefs of warlike figures such as Mars and Victory. Despite the architectural complexity, gates were often routinely installed in forts or on Hadrian's Wall even though they were not always needed. In time, changes in practice, difficult access or structural decay led to such gates falling into disuse and being blocked up (figure 20).

The late forts

The third and fourth centuries saw a new breed of fort, reflecting changes in imperial warfare as the Roman Empire moved onto the defensive. By the late third century a series of forts had been built around the east and south coasts to defend Britain from waterborne pirates. This was known as the *Litus Saxonicum*, or Saxon Shore. Later on, supplementary defences were added at vulnerable towns such as Horncastle (Lincolnshire). The result was a series of fortified compounds

21. Bastions of the west gate at the Saxon Shore fort of Pevensey (East Sussex). Built at the end of the third century or early in the fourth, these bastions marked the new style of defensive military architecture.

around much of the English and Welsh coasts.

Saxon Shore forts were different from older forts. Gate-towers and bastions projected from the fort walls, allowing defenders to use artillery against attackers trying to break down the gates. The new towers were also solid, making them strong enough to bear the artillery and withstand assault (figure 21). Similar bastions were added to town walls around the same time. However, York's river-front was embellished with a series of hollow towers at the beginning of the fourth century (figure 56).

Saxon Shore fort walls were massive and free-standing, being as much as 3 metres (10 feet) thick and 10 metres (33 feet) high. Internal banks were sometimes added to provide easy access to the rampart top. Little is known about internal buildings, but in general the walls enclosed more irregular areas, perhaps serving primarily as corrals for troops, horses and prisoners, and utilising timber buildings now hard to detect.

Britain's late-fourth-century coastal defences were reinforced by signal, or look-out, towers. Several have been found on the Yorkshire coast. An inscription (very rare for this date) from Ravenscar calls the building 'a tower and fort'. Remains of another at Scarborough show that the stone tower, over 15 metres (50 feet) wide at the base and perhaps 30 metres (100 feet) high, sat within a perimeter wall and ditch.

4
Military buildings

Headquarters (*principia*)

The headquarters formed the centrepiece of most forts (figure 22). It introduced the basilican hall – a form still used today for churches – to Britain, first in timber versions at, for example, Hod Hill. The hall formed a covered assembly area with a nave and one or two aisles focusing attention on one end, the tribunal. Chambers on one side stored the unit's records and standards. Unit valuables were stored in an underground chamber, usually vaulted and accessed by stairs leading down from the *sacellum*, the room containing the standards. Opposite, a doorway led to the open courtyard with a covered colonnade on each of the three remaining sides. The form resembles the urban forum and basilica because the functions were similar. Military architects were probably responsible for both, sometimes perhaps indirectly.

The hall's roof required substantial timber beams. The nave and aisles could be separated by a colonnade, which meant stone columns supporting arches (figure 23). Such an important building was liable to embellishment. This was where inscriptions were displayed as well as

22. Model of a second-century military headquarters building, typical of those found in forts along Hadrian's Wall and elsewhere in the northern frontier. Displayed at Segedunum Roman Fort Museum, Wallsend.

23. Housesteads fort headquarters cross-hall, looking south. The bases of the columns dividing the nave from the single aisle can be seen, as can the entrance passageway leading across the hall in the middle to the rooms at the rear where the unit standards would have been displayed and records kept.

decorative martial sculpture. It was also where a series of annual ceremonies, swearing allegiance to the emperor for example, were conducted.

The remaining accommodation structures in the fort, such as the barracks, the commandant's house and even the hospital, were essentially no more sophisticated than rows of rooms arranged either as rectangular strips, or in wings around a courtyard.

Granaries (*horrea*)

Granaries were among the most specialised military buildings. Every fort was equipped with one, or normally a pair. In some cases a fort might be given over largely to accommodate them. South Shields was converted for this purpose in the early third century, probably to act as a supply base for the northern frontier.

The granary presented four big problems: ventilation, resisting damp, controlling rodents, and withstanding lateral forces from settling grain. Timber granaries were supported on posts, detectable in the ground by several parallel rows of post-holes. Stone granaries were laid on dwarf walls with ventilation slots or pillars to create the same effect. This allowed air to circulate and made it harder for rats to enter. Buttresses along the side-walls acted against the grain as it settled in bins inside. Buttresses were sometimes massive, and building granaries in matched pairs helped each to act as a buttress to the other. Access to the granary was usually from a raised loading platform, or up steps, under a covered portico for unloading in rain. These features are extremely well preserved at Housesteads (figure 24) and Corbridge.

A granary at Benwell on Hadrian's Wall was built *c.*122–4 by the *classis Britannica*, the fleet arm of the Roman army in Britain. More usually, the legions were responsible for much fort building in the early second century. This was so much so that the Twentieth Legion had to suspend building its fortress at Chester while Hadrian's Wall and the Antonine Wall, as well as all the other northern forts, were under construction. The garrisons of almost all these frontier forts were the auxiliary infantry and cavalry units. The use of the fleet was a mark of the Roman army's flexibility. By the third century, the auxiliaries were able to undertake repairs and new building themselves, not just of granaries but of all sorts of fort buildings.

24. The northern granary at Housesteads. On the left, and in the foreground, are the buttresses to support the north and west walls. The floor supports are still in place. The granary was buttressed to the south by the southern granary.

25. The mid-first-century legionary baths at Exeter (Devon), displayed in a cutaway model at the Royal Albert Memorial Museum, Exeter.

Baths and latrines

Bathing is regarded as synonymous with Roman life, but in Britain baths and latrines are generally better known in forts than in towns and at villas. The legionary bath-house at Exeter dates to the 50s AD, when the fortress was probably a base for the Second Legion Augusta. One of the earliest major architectural works to have appeared in Britain, it covered some 4000 square metres but was modest in scale compared to legionary baths on the Continent.

The Exeter baths had vaults, apses, hypocausts, decorative stone floors and walls, and what may have been the earliest mosaic laid in Britain. This is exceptional because mosaics are generally absent from military buildings. Interestingly, the Second Legion's later base at Caerleon is one of few other Romano-British military sites to feature a mosaic. Marble was used to create decorative mouldings and veneer finishes to walls. A building like this would be worthy of note at any time, right up to the present, but in Britain in the mid first century it must have seemed extraordinary. Monumental legionary baths were also later built at Caerleon and Wroxeter (figure 25).

Channels in the stone and tile work, and recesses, show that the Exeter baths included plumbing systems using lead pipes, and bronze boilers and tanks supported on massive iron bars. Tiles would have been unable to cope with flames from the furnaces heating the boiler base. Fire was not always well controlled in baths and this is how we know about many other fort baths without having to find the actual buildings. At Bowes (Durham) an inscription of *c.*197–202 records that the Vettonian Cavalry wing rebuilt the baths for the resident First Cohort of Thracians after fire destruction.

To the ten or so inscriptions that record similar work (figure 11), we can add the physical remains of baths at numerous forts, of which the

26. The baths at Chesters fort on Hadrian's Wall as they might have appeared in the mid second century. This is a digitally manipulated image using a photograph of the working baths replica at Wallsend fort, itself based on an exact reverse image plan of the Chesters original. Here the picture has been converted to the Chesters orientation with a simulated fort wall beyond and the River Tyne in the foreground.

best preserved are those at Chesters on Hadrian's Wall (figure 26). Here, many important features mark the military bath-house as an excellent example of army architectural skills. The building was all stone with tufa barrel-vault roofs. The lateral forces caused by the vaults were resisted by buttresses, as well as by tucking the building

27. The latrine at Housesteads in the south-east corner of the fort. The building was fed by tanks, which are visible in the foreground and beyond, using a network of open conduits. The tanks were filled with rain water running off from the fort.

into a slope. The baths were located close to the river to aid drainage, and far enough from the fort to ensure that a fire did not involve the main establishment. Some idea of the scale can be gained at Wallsend, where a modern full-scale replica of the Chesters baths (but in mirror image) has been built and is fully operational (figure 26). At some military bases, including Castleford (West Yorkshire), baths were built in fort annexes, laid out alongside the fort compound with their own defences.

The best-known latrine is at Housesteads (figure 27). Drainage across this ridge-hugging fort was arranged to send water to the lowest point in the south-east corner, where the latrines were built. The latrine was conventional with open seating ranged around three walls. Below, a water channel carried waste away. Drainage and rain water gathered in cisterns close by, running down open conduits to feed the underfloor waste drain as well as a hand basin and foot-level sponge-dipping channel. Run-off from the latter went into the underfloor waste drain, which then discharged its undesirable contents through an opening in the fort wall – right into the civilian settlement beyond.

Arenas

Entertainments like gladiator bouts are regarded as defining features of Roman society. The fortresses at Chester and Caerleon and the fort at

28. The arena, *ludus*, at Caerleon. The arena was built in the late first century but was subsequently modified and repaired. The seating area was created out of eight earthen banks, revetted with stone walls and buttresses.

London had military arenas (*ludi*). At Caerleon, eight earthen banks were raised around a sunken elliptical arena. Each bank was revetted by stone walls, supported on the outside by buttressing (figure 28). Wooden seats were then laid out on the banks. Military arena entertainments featured religious festivals, mock battles and tournaments, including commemorative re-enactments of mythical battles, with the soldiers sporting face-masks and special dress uniforms to emulate legendary heroes and mythical enemies.

Dereliction

Despite the bout of rebuilding at Roman forts in the early third century, military buildings such as baths and granaries seem to have become unusual in the fourth century. The new forts of the Saxon Shore have yielded very few identifiable structures. In the northern forts deterioration set in and even the legionary fortresses seem to have decayed into semi-ruin. Only at certain forts was there any sort of building work, and that is probably attributable to local initiative. South Shields, for example, was equipped with a commandant's house of Mediterranean courtyard style in the fourth century. This was a time when fort building of almost any sort was at an end, and when the soldiers at Housesteads were propping up their derelict gates with timber.

5
Public buildings

Forum and basilica

Towns were mechanisms for government, and they integrated conquered tribes into the Roman system by allowing the local élite to retain prestige and status, though under control. All major towns were provided with civic centres, the focus of which was the forum and basilica – a showcase of Roman public architecture housing the process of law and administration, and commerce (figures 29, 30). In Britain they resembled the military headquarters, but on a larger scale.

The basilicas and forums were similar, but no two were the same. Each was the biggest investment its town would ever see, built from at least the 70s onwards. The process lasted for around the next sixty years. The complex at St Albans was dedicated in 79 or 81 under Vespasian or Titus (figure 29), and Wroxeter's in 130–3 under Hadrian.

The forum and basilica at Caerwent (Monmouthshire), capital of the

29. The forum and basilica at St Albans (Hertfordshire) as it might have appeared in the late first or the second century. On a scale matching medieval cathedrals, these great civic centres were amongst the largest structures in Roman Britain.

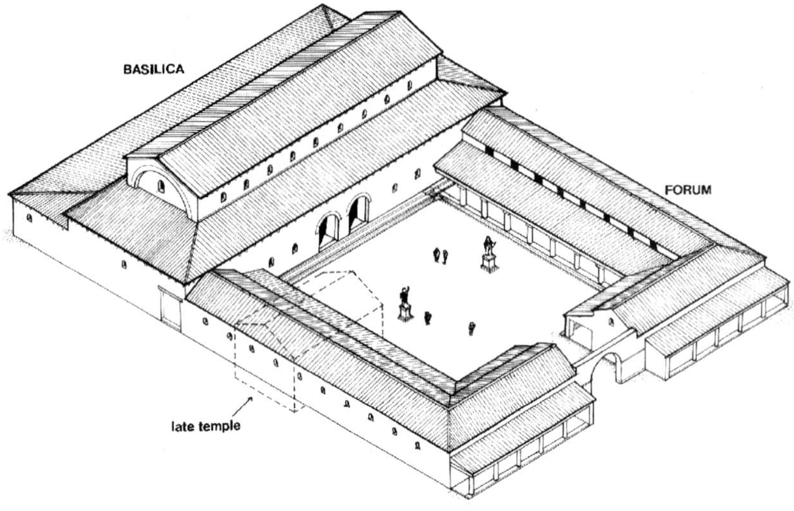

30. Reconstruction drawing of the modest forum and basilica at Caerwent (Monmouthshire). All the features exhibited by the bigger versions are present. Late in its history, a temple-like structure was inserted in the west wing.

Silurian tribal region, is an excellent example of how even a small and remote tribal centre was equipped with civic architecture that someone from any part of the Empire would have recognised (figure 30). This had proved a difficult part of Britain to suppress, and the town was only a few miles from the legionary fortress at Caerleon.

The Caerwent forum was small – the piazza was just 1023 square metres, whereas London's was close to 10,000 square metres. The basilica was the size of a reasonable parish church. At least one end (the east) had a raised tribunal where civic and provincial authorities would have sat to pronounce on matters of law (figure 4). Another row of rooms, in which records were stored, flanked the north aisle. The largest room was probably where the local senate of officials, qualified by property, met to govern the region. Unlike the rest of the basilica, it was embellished with a small mosaic and painted walls.

The Caerwent forum was on the south side of the basilica (normal but not universal). It opened off the main street through the town so that a visitor could walk in and see the basilica. A portico lined the street. Inside, the three sides of the forum had more porticoes and shops within. The piazza, kept dry by a drainage system, would have been filled with stalls and traders, scattered amongst the statues of emperors and worthies.

Theatres

St Albans is the only Romano-British town in which substantial physical remains of a theatre have been found, though its form is unusual and not truly classical like the examples at Canterbury and Colchester, identified from traces. The St Albans theatre resembled a truncated amphitheatre (figures 9, 28). It must have been used both for conventional stage plays and displays in the orchestra. The theatre here, as was common, was next to a large temple because theatrical displays of myth and religious ceremony played the most important part in temple ritual. This may explain why the theatre was derelict by the fourth century, once Christianity became legally enforced – this would have been very effective in a town where settlement had probably started to drift east around the grave of the Christian martyr Alban, which almost certainly lies under the medieval abbey church.

Public baths

The greatest surviving remains of buildings in Roman towns in Britain are the baths at Leicester, Wroxeter and Bath itself (figures 13, 31, 32). Leicester's and Wroxeter's baths were built in the mid second century

31. Wroxeter (Shropshire). The view is north across the baths complex to the wall of the basilican exercise hall (similar to the government basilica). The entrance to the hall is still in place. This second-century establishment lay across the road from the forum and basilica, with its vaulted halls being the most complex structures in the town.

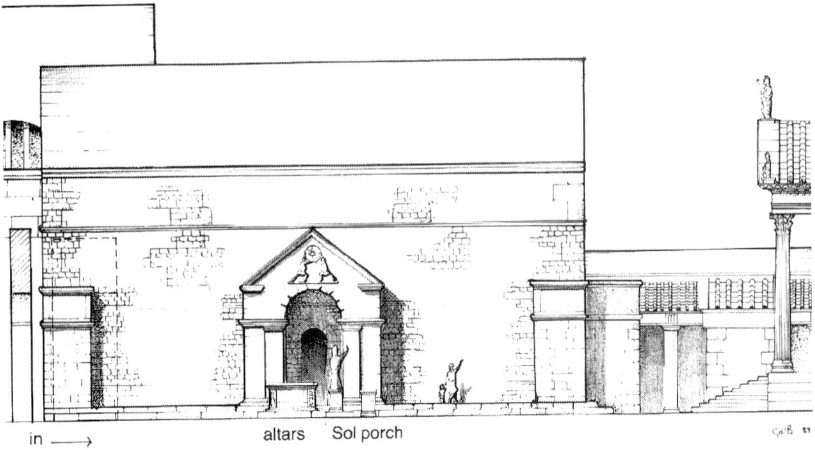

32. The temple precinct at Bath (Somerset), looking south towards the vaulted cover building over the sacred spring. Behind, to the left, is the end of the vault covering the Great Bath. On the right are the steps and façade of the temple of Sulis-Minerva.

as part of their roles as civitas capitals of the Corieltauvi and the Cornovii tribal regions respectively. Each complex included a basilican structure, adapted to create a covered exercise hall or *palaestra*. In warmer climates the *palaestra* was an open area surrounded by colonnades – obviously unsuitable in Britain. The remainder of the baths retained the conventional series of *frigidarium* (cold), *tepidarium* (warm) and *caldarium* (hot) rooms. Vaults made it possible to create large roofed areas, vented by huge openings. Like most major public baths, they were near the forum and formed a vital part of Roman commercial and social life. Business friendships and deals were made in the baths, where men of substance could hold court in discreet surroundings.

Bath (*Aquae Sulis*, 'The Waters of Sulis') was a healing spa built around a hot spring, sacred to the god Sulis. The focus was the sacred spring where hot waters bubbled out of the soil (figure 32). One possibility is that the army developed the place as a recreational centre for troops (known to have been done on the Continent). The large number of military tombstones and altars found here favours this interpretation.

In its late-second-century heyday the Bath spring was covered over with its own vaulted building, designed to emulate a dark and mysterious cave. Here visitors could throw in offerings to the god. Clustering around it were the main baths straggling off to the south-east. Fragments of architectural carvings make it very likely that lesser temples, including a *tholos*, lay nearby, as well as perhaps a theatre (see chapter 6).

Ornamental buildings

Towns were also decorated with more ornamental structures, including arches and columns. Monumental arches represented symbolic gateways from one place to another and served as 'notice boards' for imperial bragging and plinths for statues (figure 33). Some were installed at special, non-urban locations. Richborough, later to become a Saxon Shore fort, enjoyed a period from the late first century when a vast triumphal arch, clad in Italian marble, formed the honorific entrance to the province of Britain. Unfortunately, only its foundations and a scattering of its adornment survive, left behind when it was knocked down to make way for the late-third-century fort. Foundations of arches have also turned up in a few towns, including London, where they acted as entrances to temple compounds, and St Albans, where several stood astride the main road through the town. Several more are recorded on inscriptions, even from the little town at Ancaster (Lincolnshire), showing that they must once have been far more widespread. Examples from Italy show what they might have looked like (figure 33).

33. (Left) The Arch of Titus at Rome provides a reasonable idea of the original appearance of the triumphal arch at Richborough (though this had a lateral passage through the piers), which was also clad in Italian marble.
(Right) This brick arch at Pompeii, Italy, has lost its marble facing but it was one of several that stood astride the city streets providing commemorative and symbolic entrances to zones. In Britain, St Albans is known to have had several like it and inscriptions record others.

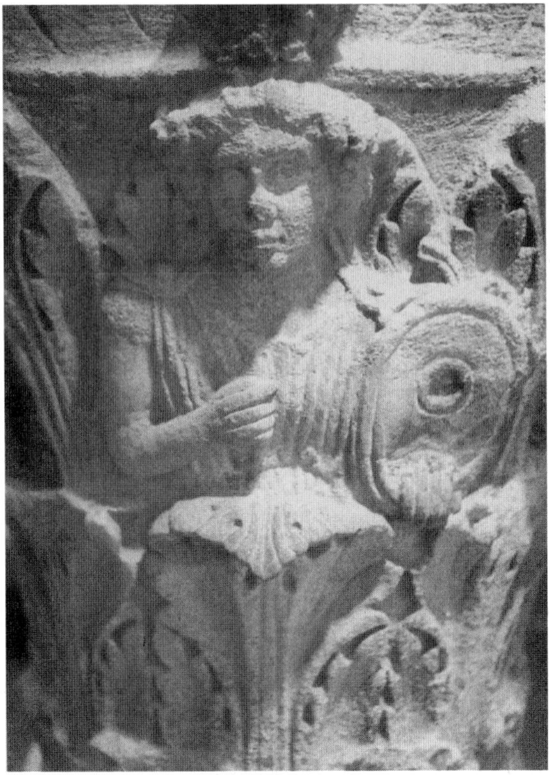

34. Capital from a Jupiter column at Cirencester (Gloucestershire), depicting Bacchus. Other figures from Bacchic myth appear on the other three sides. A base from another column from the town can be dated to the early fourth century and this may be contemporary.

Jupiter columns have also turned up in several places, with two from Cirencester being particularly well known. Uncompromisingly pagan, these were free-standing columns situated in prominent public places. The column capital could be one of the most elaborately designed pieces of sculpture in the town (figure 34), and on top would have been a figure of Jupiter hurling thunderbolts.

Town walls

External walls and gates (see page 7) are often the only visible remains of Roman towns in Britain. Useful to medieval townsfolk, they have frequently been repaired and reused right up to early modern times. Even the abandoned town at Silchester (Hampshire) has a virtually complete circuit. As well as being defensive, walls help control land use, exclude rural groups or tribes considered undesirable, provide supervision of trade for taxes and create an imposing image of power.

35. The walls and bastions of Caerwent (Monmouthshire), looking west along the south face.

Although earthen banks were used in the first and second centuries, the main phase of urban stone walls did not begin until the late second and early third centuries. Sometimes this involved incorporating existing free-standing monumental gateways, for example at Colchester.

Urban walls started to resemble the Saxon Shore forts in the fourth century when bastions were added to many of them. Caerwent's are the most impressive today (figure 35), but excavations in London's bastions show that existing monuments, including tombs, were torn down to provide stone. While the bastions were being built, the great public buildings of earlier periods were derelict. The theatre at St Albans was filled with rubbish, and the exercise hall of Wroxeter's great baths was in ruins. It is possible that towns had become in effect part of the fort system, with soldiers or private armies directing modifications for defence. The truth is that we do not know, but by the early fifth century almost all the public buildings in Roman towns were entirely obsolete – even the bastions.

6
Temples, shrines and tombs

Roman inscriptions from Britain record more temples and shrines than any other class of building in the province, adding to those known from excavations. Temples normally lay within a *temenos* enclosure where public ceremony took place. Depending on whether this was in the countryside or in a town, and the nature of the cult, a *temenos* might just have simple rooms and entranceways or elaborate complexes of buildings, including dormitories, baths and subsidiary temples. At the fourth-century shrine complex to Nodens at Lydney (Gloucestershire) the *temenos* sprawled across an old Iron Age hillfort and included facilities to accommodate pilgrims (figure 38).

Romano-Celtic temples

The standard Romano-British type was what we call the Romano-Celtic temple. This consisted usually of a square *cella*, surrounded by an ambulatory. Many are known in Britain, and they were often extended with flanking chambers, for example at Lamyatt Beacon (Somerset). Excavation at many sites, for example at Harlow (Essex), shows that Iron Age temples of circular form often turn up underneath or close by. This is an interesting parallel to some villa sites (see chapter 7).

Romano-Celtic temples remained in use right into the fourth century, supposedly when Christianity was pre-eminent. But communities in

36. The fourth-century temple at Maiden Castle (Dorset), with, to the right, adjacent priest's house and possible kiosk for sales of votive goods.

37. The temple of Sulis-Minerva at Bath (Somerset), looking west across the temple precinct.

remoter provinces often clung on to old customs. The establishment of rural temples in Britain peaked in the fourth century, even though urban temples were falling into disuse. The emperor Julian (360–3) tried to revive paganism. Like many of his contemporaries, he regarded the old gods as symbolic of the 'good old days' when Rome's power was unchallenged.

Many new temples were built close to the great fourth-century villas, themselves often decorated with elaborate mosaics depicting pagan myth. Ancient locations such as old hillforts were chosen for some. Perhaps this was the attraction at Maiden Castle (Dorset), close to the Roman town of *Durnovaria* (modern Dorchester). On the Iron Age hillfort a new temple of Romano-Celtic design was built in the fourth century, and a priest's house stood close by (figure 36).

Classical temples

Classical temples were rare in Roman Britain. With their façades of steps leading up to columns supporting a pediment, and the *cella* where the image of the god or goddess was stored, they exemplify Roman religious architecture.

The earliest erected was the temple of Claudius at Colchester, destroyed in the year 60 during the Boudican Revolt. The temple was rebuilt, but now only its concrete podium and vaults survive, used by the Normans for the foundations of Colchester Castle. Since classical temples were built to strict rules and proportions it is possible to have a good idea of what the temple once looked like (figure 3).

The temple of Sulis-Minerva at Bath is much better known, although most of it remains buried. Eighteenth-century clearance revealed much of the temple's collapsed façade, showing that it was a vibrant mix of classical and Romano-British styles. The temple was classical tetrastyle, but the pediment contained a dramatic carving of a Gorgon's head, symbolising the local deity Sulis. A statue of Sulis's classical counterpart, Minerva, stood within the *cella*. What makes this temple so pleasing is how it overlooked the intimate temple precinct with its central altar and surrounding carved reliefs, making an elegant and charming zone. With the honey-coloured Bath stone, and colourfully painted altars and statues, it must have resembled a grotto (figure 37).

Basilican temples

The basilica also proved adaptable for churches and certain temples, preserving the form down to our time (figures 4, 38, 39). Very few churches are known from Roman Britain and even those that are have been identified by building type and location rather than by any Christian artefacts found. The basilican temples to the Persian mystery god Mithras, *mithraea*, are much better known, examples having been found on

38. The shrine complex at Lydney (Gloucestershire). The temple stands on its own at the left. To the right was accommodation for pilgrims, and in the background a bath suite. (After Wheeler)

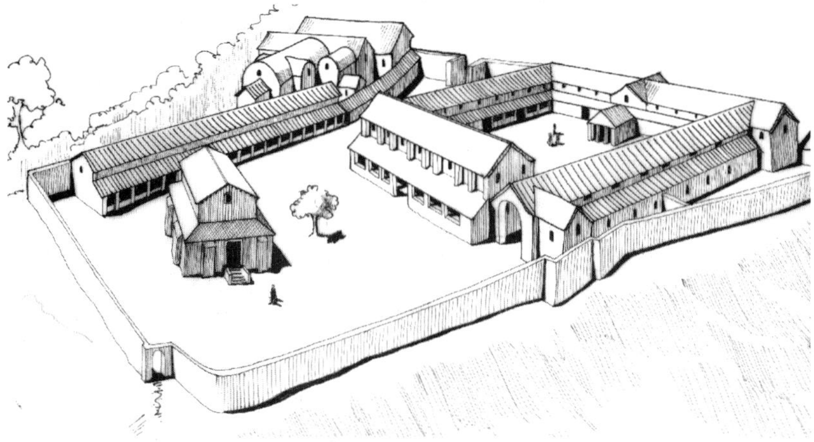

39. The *mithraeum* at Carrawburgh on Hadrian's Wall. The basilican-style nave runs down the middle. Modern concrete posts mark the wooden pillars separating the aisles and supporting the roof. The altars (modern reproductions) were once overlooked by a scene of Mithras slaying the sacred bull.

Hadrian's Wall, at Caernarfon and in London. The cults seem very different but their popularity reflected a common interest in Eastern religions promising redemption through participation in sacred meals. Mithraism, however, was open only to men and was especially popular amongst soldiers. Even the London example contained reliefs provided by a veteran of the Second Legion.

The best explored is the *mithraeum* from the fort at Carrawburgh on Hadrian's Wall; it is the only British example visible in its original location (figure 39). It began life as a simple stone rectangle but was extended, and an apse added, while two lines of timber columns inside created a *narthex*, nave and aisles and supported the roof. Windowless and small, the *mithraeum* was designed to recreate the cave in which Mithras slew the sacred bull, a depiction of which was set up in the apse along with several altars. It even featured an ordeal pit by the entrance where participants could be temporarily buried as a test of endurance.

The temple of Antenociticus at Benwell, further east along the Wall, was even simpler. This consisted of a masonry chamber and apse, containing the god's cult statue, flanked by a pair of altars (figure 40). Dating to the late second century, and having a short life, it was built by

40. The temple of Antenociticus at Benwell on Hadrian's Wall, showing the apse containing a base for the statue of the god and flanked by altars.

Roman soldiers to pay their respects to a god who must have been venerated locally before the army arrived.

Churches are generally devoid of any artefacts or inscriptions and the so-called church at Silchester has defied definitive identification since it faces west rather than east. Only the cemetery 'church' outside the walls at Colchester can reasonably be identified as a probable Christian building. Surrounded by east–west graves, it might lie over a martyr's grave. But no church of Roman date can be identified with absolute certainty in Britain.

Other temples

At Nettleton, not far from Bath, a late-first-century circular temple was replaced in the mid third century by an extraordinary successor based on concentric octagons. Essentially an elaboration of the Romano-Celtic design (above), this involved a central octagonal vaulted cult chamber opening on to a series of radiating chambers, one of which acted as the entrance (figure 41). The designer of the building, and the managers of the cult here (known from an altar to have been to Apollo), had an eye for what is still today a beautiful small valley, through which the trans-Britannia trunk route we call the Fosse Way ran. Nettleton had

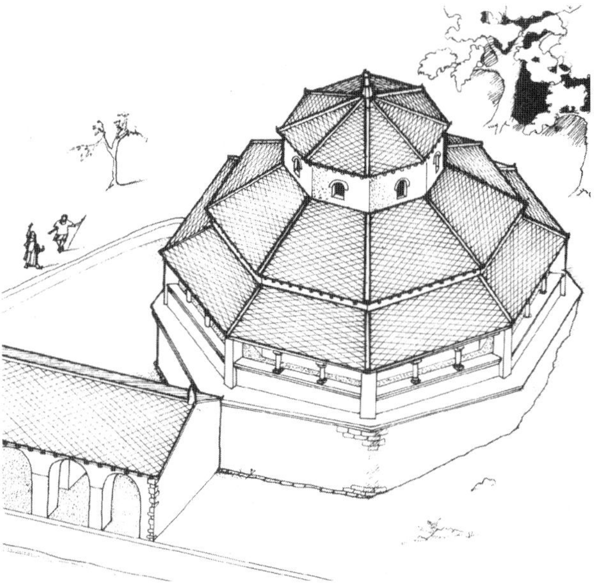

41. The octagonal temple of Apollo at Nettleton (Wiltshire) as it may have appeared in the late third century. The central lantern placed enormous stress on the supporting walls and the failure to include buttresses had disastrous consequences. By the mid fourth century the temple was partly derelict.

everything a cult needed – a god, aesthetics and communications. The cult centre prospered from the passing trade, and the small settlement developed as facilities grew up to service visitors and their needs.

Nettleton's architect made a fundamental mistake. The central chamber with its vaults pushed down and outwards. The sixth-century church of San Vitale at Ravenna in Italy has a similar plan and it still stands because the builders included vast buttresses to counteract these forces. Without buttresses, the Nettleton temple started to collapse. In *c.*300 hasty steps were taken to arrest the damage, and arches in some radial walls were filled. It was to no avail and the temple continued to disintegrate. By the mid fourth century it was partially derelict but cult activity continued amongst the debris before the vaults finally collapsed altogether.

Equally remarkable, but much better built, was the strange beehive building known as 'Arthur's O'on' at Carron, north of the Antonine Wall. Tantalising records suggest it was a temple, perhaps dedicated to Victory or Jupiter, that survived until the eighteenth century, when it was destroyed for building stone (figure 5). The design was extremely stable because it efficiently transmitted forces from the domed roof down through the walls. A window in the south side was probably devised to let the sun shine on the cult statue within. We will never know.

42. The Littlecote (Wiltshire) villa and triconch hall in the fourth century. The hall, containing an Orpheus mosaic, was either an elaborate dining hall or perhaps a cult centre. Opinion is divided.

The triple-apsed (triconch) hall at Littlecote (Wiltshire) is a mystery (figure 42). This was once an ordinary barn, standing a few yards from the villa house. Looking very much like a church from the Eastern Empire with its three apses, cross-hall and nave, it is impossible to know if this was a hall for an Orphic cult (represented on its mosaic floor) or just a dramatic dining room, similar to one in a contemporary Roman palace at Piazza Armerina in Sicily. The architect produced a pleasing symmetrical design yet made the strange mistake of building it partly over a filled-in ditch of the adjacent road. As a result, the hall suffered cracking and some subsidence.

At Lydney (Gloucestershire) the cult centre was built in the fourth century on an Iron Age hillfort like Maiden Castle (figures 36, 38). Nodens was worshipped as a healing god with practices originating in Greece at shrines of Asklepios. The central experience was sleeping in the presence of the god, often in a drugged or drunken state, in the hope of a visitation in a dream and a cure. To make this possible, the temple design merged Romano-Celtic and basilican forms. Niches in the ambulatory acted as little bedchambers. Unfortunately for the builders, a fault under one of the *cella* piers caused the temple to suffer a major collapse. Rebuilding replaced the piers with solid walls.

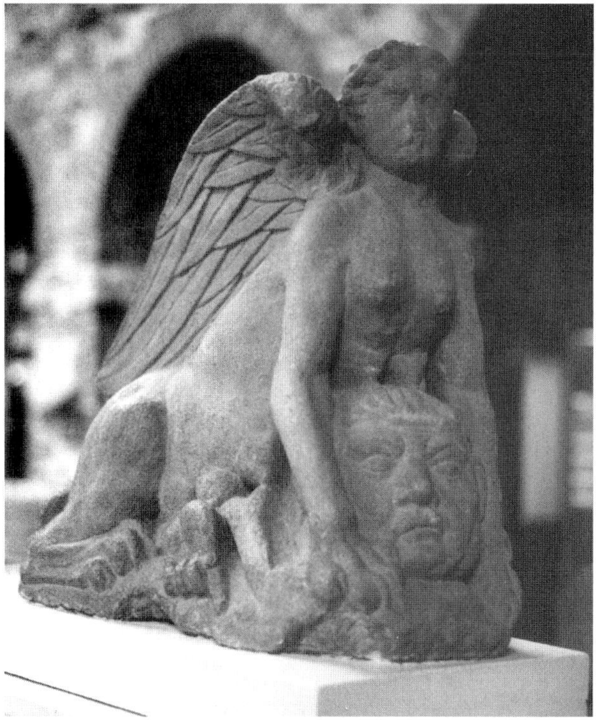

43. Sculpture of a sphinx with a captive victim. Such motifs were common decorative features of elaborate tombs and can help identify the building's purpose. Found at Colchester (Essex).

Tombs

Substantial Roman tombs are rare in Britain though sculptures of lions devouring victims or sphinxes – standard tomb embellishments – show they existed at Corbridge, Colchester and near Water Newton (figure 43). Large tombs normally took the form of earth cores, revetted by walls sometimes supported with buttresses, and capped with mounds decorated with trees or sculpture, like that close to the villa at Keston (Kent). Surviving examples are all reduced to their lower courses, and one seems to have been integrated into a small post-Roman Christian chapel at Stone-by-Faversham (Kent). But the so-called 'temple-mausoleum' at Lullingstone villa (Kent) shows that tombs could be more elaborate. Here, two young adults were buried in lead coffins in a pit dug on the hillside overlooking the villa. The pit was sealed and a vaulted building, resembling a Romano-Celtic temple, erected over it. This probably provided the residents with the chance to venerate various ancestors, perhaps displayed as statues. The recovery of two second-century male busts from a cellar in the house itself, where they had been sealed, may be connected.

7
Houses and villas

Town houses and rural villas were the least sophisticated architectural forms in Roman Britain. In general, villas were just rows of rooms linked by corridors. Roman-type housing is defined by the appearance of rectangular plans, together with features including mosaics, painted wall plaster, hypocausts, tiled roofs, window glass, and architectural decoration such as finials, balustrades or columns. From the mid first century AD, simple examples started to supplant existing housing, but the process of development was slow, with few rural houses being significantly elaborated for another century (figure 44). Roundhouses of Iron Age type remained in widespread use, often as subsidiary components of villa estates perhaps occupied by workers.

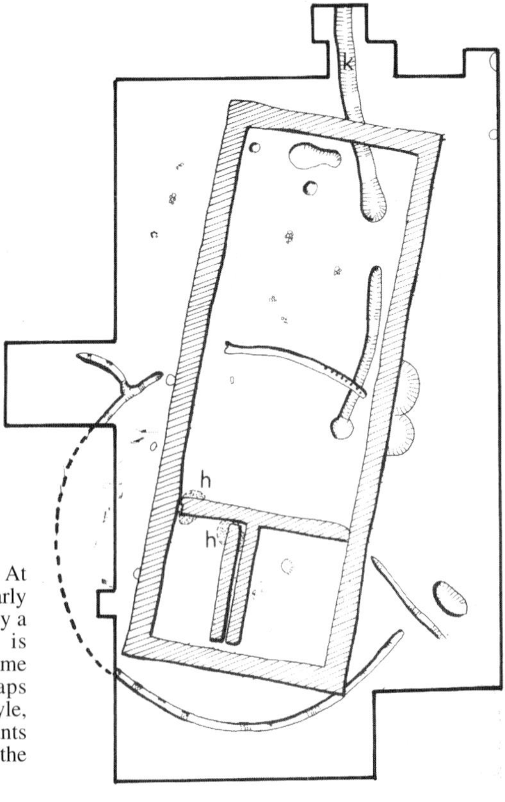

44. Upward mobility or eviction? At Quinton (Northamptonshire) the early roundhouse has been supplanted by a rectangular stone house. It is impossible to say whether the same people were responsible, perhaps seeking a more Romanised lifestyle, or whether the original inhabitants were evicted and new people took the site. (After Taylor)

Villas

The great villas of the countryside, most of which had existed in modest form since the second century, were not usually subjected to major improvements until the late third century. This is what makes the house at Fishbourne near Chichester (West Sussex) so remarkable (figure 10). As early as the reign of Nero (54–68), a substantial house with baths and sophisticated decoration was erected on a site previously occupied by military-type timber buildings. The owner is unknown – as is the case for every other Roman house in Britain – but the Fishbourne house probably belonged either to the Roman governor of the province or the first-century puppet pro-Roman tribal king of the area, Tiberius Claudius Togidubnus (also known as Cogidubnus).

In the 70s, the Neronian house was replaced by a much bigger version built in four wings around a large ornamental garden, together with other extensions. The new 'palace' had a monumental entrance leading through the gardens, overlooked by north and south wings, to a room interpreted as an audience chamber. The building was destroyed in a late-third-century fire but excavations revealed that Fishbourne had been designed by a master architect and fitted out by an army of artisans with columns, carved capitals, exotic stone veneers, mosaic floors and painted wall plaster.

Until the late third century, Romano-British rural housing usually consisted of nothing more imposing than 'winged-corridor' houses. These consisted of a simple row of rooms and a corridor, with a wing at one or both ends, creating usually a roughly symmetrical façade. Containing rooms used as a kitchen, bedrooms, living rooms, stores and sometimes a modest bath suite, many examples are known but the house at Redlands Farm, Stanwick (Northamptonshire) is exceptional because of the collapsed sections of wall.

The Stanwick house started life as a mill. This building formed the central wing of the later villa, with new wall divisions creating several rooms. One of these contained a hypocaust and another a mosaic. A corridor was tacked on, as well as a pair of wings. This is very interesting because the normal route was to start off as a row of rooms. This shows that the Romano-British house builder wanted to conform to a stereotype design. The house ended up as shown in figure 45. The reconstruction is probably more accurate than usual because the wings were demolished in the late fourth century after one started subsiding into the filled-in water channel, which once drove the mill wheel. One gable end was left where it fell, preserving exactly how the wall had been built. The collapsed gable shows that the house had an upper storey, accessed by what may have been an external stairway.

The basic form of the Redlands Farm house is not in doubt but it

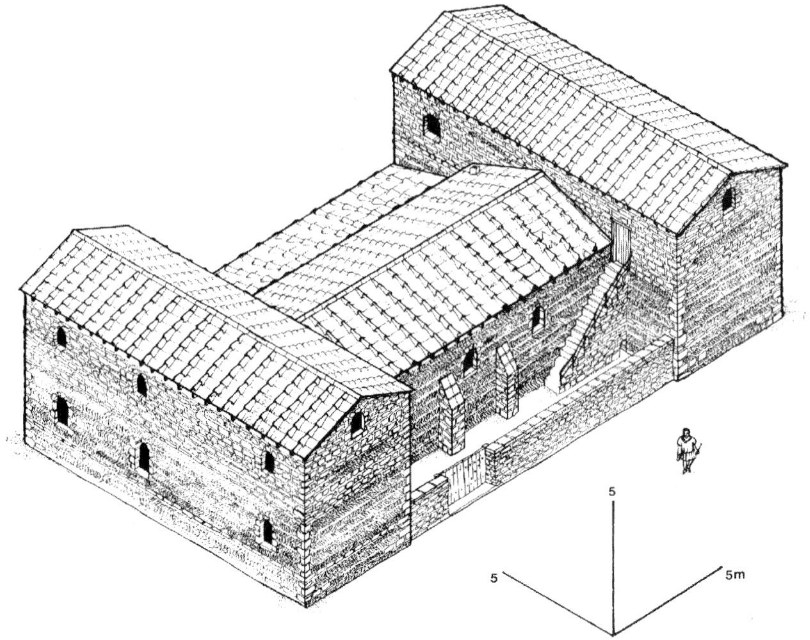

45. This winged-corridor villa at Redlands Farm, Stanwick (Northamptonshire), started off as a mill. The mill was adapted to form the core of a house, to which a pair of wings was added. Collapsed walling has allowed an unusual degree of accuracy in reconstructing the house on paper.

would be a mistake to assume that similar plans necessarily meant similar buildings. One possibility is that these wings in some cases were actually towers, known from wall paintings on the Continent and in North Africa to have been used (figure 8).

Redlands Farm was not unusual in lasting right into the fourth century as a winged-corridor villa. At some villas, this phase was followed by dramatic extension of the wings to create three wings, sometimes joined by a fourth. This of course does not represent any more complex architecture but was clearly an exercise in display of wealth and enhancement of lifestyle. The well-known villa at Bignor (West Sussex) is almost an archetype for the process. Here, the third-century winged-corridor villa was extended to integrate extant barns and outbuildings including baths (thus taking a substantial risk if fire broke out) into a single structure. Behind this essentially symmetrical core, additional chambers and rooms were built on. Some of these additional rooms featured floors laid with the exceptional series of polychrome mosaics

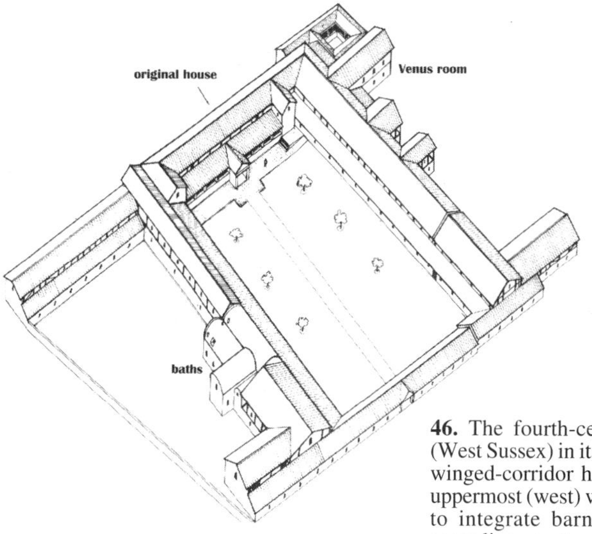

46. The fourth-century house at Bignor (West Sussex) in its final form. The original winged-corridor house can be seen in the uppermost (west) wing. Extension of wings to integrate barns and baths created a sprawling courtyard villa.

that were an integral part of the house's finest phase (figure 46).

It is usually assumed that large villas like Bignor were the focal point of rural estates, with wealth founded in farming. They were perhaps owned by members of local tribal aristocracies who manipulated local economies to their advantage through the tribal council of their region, benefiting from a gradual accumulation of wealth to finance improvements to their houses. It is equally possible that owners included immigrants, wealthy military veterans, or absentee landlords who lived on the Continent and let their property to tenants.

Some villas had unusual features (figures 47, 48). This has led to a theory that they may have had unexpected functions, perhaps as accommodation for cult pilgrims. Unfortunately, there is no evidence for this. Letters and documents written elsewhere in the Roman world show that it was normal to include temples and grottoes in villa gardens. Some villa owners took responsibility for ancient cults established on their estates, regarding it as a privilege and a duty of rank.

Great Witcombe (Gloucestershire) is extremely unusual (figure 47). Lying on a steep slope riddled with streams, the site looks hopelessly unsuitable for a house. But the location is extremely beautiful, reflecting the Roman love of delightful settings. To cope with the terrain, the house was designed around a narrow central wing buttressed to resist subsidence. At either end, much more substantial wings were terraced into the slope, with a bath suite on one end. While the streams might be

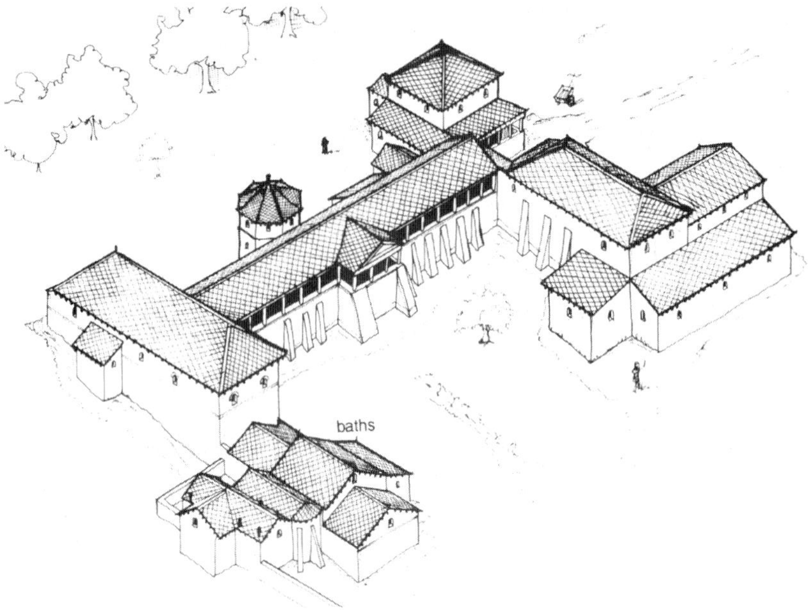

47. The curiously designed fourth-century house at Great Witcombe (Gloucestershire) lay on a hillside over a number of streams. It has been suggested that this was the centre of a water-deity shrine but it is no less possible that the owner built his house into the landscape, recognising a beauty spot for what it was, and still is.

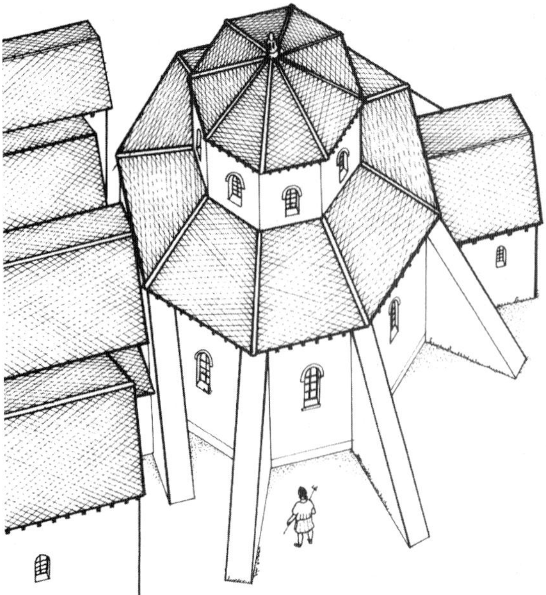

48. The ostentatious and ambitious octagonal *frigidarium* at Lufton (Somerset) was the most conspicuous part of the house. Its architect recognised the importance of buttressing (see figure 41).

49. Decorative features.
(Above) Stone balustrade from the house at Chedworth (Gloucestershire). This would probably have lined a veranda overlooking the garden.
(Right) Column stump from Bignor (West Sussex). This would have supported an open portico around the garden or courtyard.

evidence for a water-nymph cult, manipulation of water was integral to the Roman concept of decorative architecture and could also play an important role in providing food refrigeration – testified in the fifth-century letters of a wealthy Gallo-Roman called Sidonius. But it would also have been quite normal to create a cult around the place as a means to enhance its attraction and exotic appeal.

Lufton (Somerset) villa was built on a virgin site in the late third century (figure 48). Here the octagonal form, utilised at Nettleton for a temple, was the basis of an imposing *frigidarium* in the villa's baths. Unlike the Nettleton architect, the Lufton designer appreciated in time the consequence of supporting a lantern and installed large buttresses to hold the building up. The baths here are a reminder that some wealthy Romans were given to showing off their wealth in the most ostentatious way possible, just as their modern counterparts build extravagant swimming pools or sun lounges.

Chedworth (Gloucestershire) has remained one of Britain's best-known villas. A number of architectural features have survived here, showing that the easily carved Cotswold stone was exploited to provide balustrades and columns, decorating open verandas and colonnades (figure 49).

Town houses

Towns like London and St Albans experienced rapid phases of

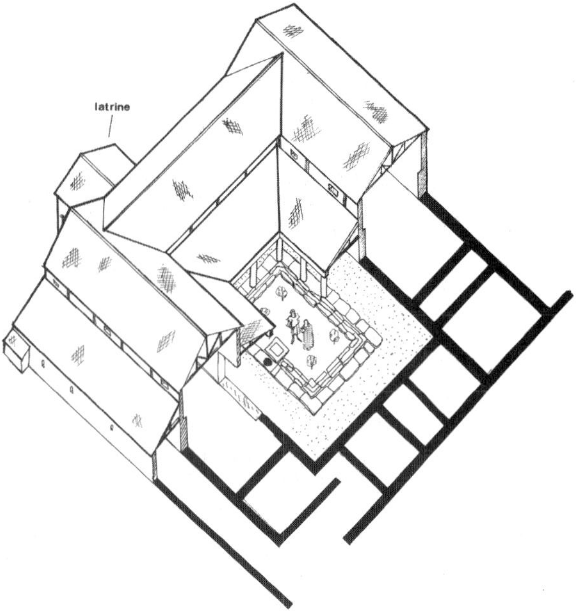

50. A town house from Caerwent (Monmouthshire). Unlike the sprawling villas of the countryside, this has been built to look inwards, recalling Mediterranean houses where seclusion and shade were priorities. Perhaps built by, or for, a legionary veteran from nearby Caerleon whose original home was Italy, Spain, Gaul or North Africa.

expansion during the late first century and into the second century. But many of the houses were simple strip buildings of timber and wattle and daub, clustering along street frontages in a relatively haphazard fashion. At Colchester, the early colony made use of the old fortress barracks for housing.

Problems with fire contributed to the introduction of stone houses, which resemble the villas except that pressure on space meant cellars were quite common. Few town houses grew beyond the winged-corridor stage, but some conform to the type of Mediterranean-style house ranging around a small inner courtyard surrounded by a colonnade. This type of house is well known at places like Pompeii in Italy and was ideal for creating a peaceful and intimate home looking inwards rather than

51. The façade from the gable end of the fourth-century aisled villa at Meonstoke (Hampshire), showing a blind arcade created from bricks to produce a decorative effect. Below was a row of clerestory windows. Now displayed in the British Museum. See also figure 52.

52. A reconstructed view of an aisled Roman house similar to the Meonstoke house (figure 51). Digitally adapted from an image of a seventeenth- or eighteenth-century house in Werrington, Peterborough, which bears a convenient resemblance to the Roman form, though a number of features have been added here, and others, including chimneys, removed.

outwards, and sheltering the owners from the blazing sun. Obviously, Britain was not an ideal place for this, but conservatism or a desire to appear more sophisticated may have been responsible for examples at places like Caerwent, probably lived in by some veterans from the nearby legionary fortress at Caerleon (figure 50).

Town houses were built in very small numbers in the fourth century. One of the curiosities of Roman Britain is the apparent decline in urban life. A fourth-century house at Cirencester is one of the few examples of late date. But outbuildings and finds make it very likely this was actually a working farm, reflecting a trend elsewhere for fewer houses to occupy larger and larger plots of land within town walls.

Aisled houses

The basilican form returns once more to show that it was the most flexible building design in Roman Britain. Its great advantage was that the interior could be arranged and rearranged at will. Aisled buildings thus served as houses, combined houses and barns, houses with animal living quarters, or just as barns. They turn up as individual homes or as subsidiary buildings associated with more elaborate villas. The site at Meonstoke (Hampshire) suffered collapse of one gable end, like Redlands Farm (see above), and this allowed archaeologists to recover a complete section of decorative brickwork – which shows that even less sophisticated buildings could be skilfully enhanced in a way normally impossible to guess from excavations of foundations and footings (figure 51). Meonstoke has shown that Roman Britain's villas may have had highly decorated exteriors, belying their essentially simple architecture.

8
Bridges, waterworks and lighthouses

Bridges and dams

Every part of Britain is criss-crossed with rivers and streams. Because timber normally decomposes we do not know how much use the Romans made of wooden bridges. Unusual circumstances at Aldwincle (Northamptonshire) preserved the remains of a wooden bridge built on 0.5 metre deep timber piles in iron sheaths, while excavations in London have shown that the first London Bridge was built *c.*100 on timber piers.

Masonry bridges are known only in the north and on Hadrian's Wall, mainly at Chesters and Willowford (figure 53). The bridge at Chesters, across the North Tyne, originated *c.*122 on eight small stone piers, with a stone or wooden superstructure carrying the frontier and a walkway across. In the early third century the structure was massively enlarged by the building of three much bigger piers, at least one of which incorporates a Hadrianic predecessor. The scattered traces of superstructure, including columns, show that this was a masonry road

53. The early-third-century eastern bridge abutment at Chesters on Hadrian's Wall. The pier supported a bridge that carried a road and the northern frontier across the river North Tyne. The earlier, Hadrianic pier can be discerned as a lozenge shape of blocks in the centre left.

bridge designed as a *tour-de-force* example of Roman bridge engineering.

Traces of a similar bridge survive at Willowford, but the remains to the south at Piercebridge (Durham) have proved controversial. Here a series of possible bridge piers sits on a stone platform. Despite being made of massive blocks, storm damage has made interpretation difficult, as has the assumed movement of the river Tees some yards to the north. One theory is that this might have been part of a large dam-and-weir system, designed to improve the navigability of rivers in the frontier-fort system. The answer is that nobody knows and current archaeology has yet conclusively to explain a very curious set of remains.

Mills

Water power was of great importance in a world without mechanisation and was enhanced by making the water pour through a narrowing channel controlled by sluice gates. Such a flow could be harnessed to turn a vertical wooden waterwheel connected through a series of gears to machinery contained within a mill, sometimes housed in a bridge pier. Both undershot and overshot types of waterwheel were used in Roman Britain. The machinery drove a large millstone for grinding grain, or might have been adapted to operate wheels for grinding metal or hammers for metalworking.

The bridges at Chesters and Willowford might have had mills, with the latter having to be modified as the river eroded westwards, but it is possible that the surviving sluices were used only for control of water-flow through the bridge (figure 53). Mills were also built as free-standing structures by rivers or artificial channels cut across bends, like the one at Haltwhistle Burn near Greatchesters fort, or that close to the shrine and village at Nettleton (see also figure 45).

Aqueducts

The Romans needed enormous quantities of water, not just for supplying towns and forts, but also for mines like Dolaucothi (Carmarthenshire), where a constant supply was needed for washing and dissolving ores. Moving water is best done with gravity and that means maintaining a gradient so that the water runs steadily from its source. The simplest methods are to cut open channels, or to lay pipes made of wood, lead or earthenware, in the ground, using natural contours wherever possible. In this way, water could be carried from a spring to a settlement or industrial establishment, even if that meant following a circuitous route. This is the commonest sort of aqueduct. For example, Greatchesters fort was fed by an open channel, cut more than a metre deep into surrounding hill slopes. At 6 miles (10 km) in length it was more than double the direct distance of the spring from the fort. Even villas had hydraulic systems. Woodchester seems to have had a stone conduit carrying water from a stream right into the villa complex. Remarkably it still works and feeds a modern pond.

Sometimes terrain created more serious problems. Roman engineers were accustomed to cutting tunnels through hills, but it was more likely that for part of the route they would have to carry the water supply across a dip or valley. In these cases the water channel had to be suspended on a solid wall, *substructio*, suitable for low heights, or a masonry arcade – the classic form of the Roman aqueduct. The last part of the Greatchesters aqueduct, now lost, was probably a *substructio*. Monumental masonry aqueducts were rare in Britain because water is so readily available that it was not often necessary to resort to such a solution.

At Lincoln, a masonry aqueduct of uncertain form carried water from a source up to 20 miles (32 km) away. The exact source remains unknown and there may have been pumping arrangements to raise the water high enough to run down the aqueduct. This, or another, may have fed a large masonry cistern installed at the north, the highest, end of the town, providing a head of water for the town baths and water supply.

54. Part of the wharf at London in Lower Thames Street, built about the end of the first century. The wharves were built out of colossal timber frames, packed with sand and rubbish. Behind them were warehouses and other harbour facilities.

Wharves

The ancient river Thames in London was much wider than now, because modern embankments restricted the river to a deeper and narrower channel. This has preserved Roman quays under later levels, allowing them to be excavated. Vast frames made of beams trimmed from mature oaks were laid across piles sunk into the riverbed and braced with more timber running back into the riverbank behind (figure 54). Although fresh trees were used, at least one timber was stamped for a military auxiliary unit so it may have been recycled from a nearby military building or fort. The areas between the timber frames were filled with gravel, sand, rock, tile and rubbish to create a level work surface on to which freight could be unloaded and transported to warehouses at the rear. Wharves have been found elsewhere in Britain, but the London examples are the best known.

Lighthouses

The seas around Britain's coasts have carried maritime traffic for thousands of years and have always been dangerous to seafarers. On the

55. The eastern lighthouse, *pharos*, at Dover, now within the grounds of Dover Castle. The lower three sections are of Roman build. The lighthouse was at least twice this height originally. It owes its survival to being converted into a bell-tower for the adjacent church.

cross-Channel route to Dover ships of the *classis Britannica* (the Roman military fleet of Britain) came in to dock at wharves near the second-century fleet fort, and later Saxon Shore fort, under modern Dover. A lighthouse (*pharos*) stood on a hill on either side of the harbour to guide ships in during foul weather or darkness (figure 55). Fuelled only by braziers, the light cannot have been very bright but, on towers up to 25 metres (80 feet) in height, they must have been prominent enough to be useful. One of the lighthouses still stands, with Roman masonry surviving to a height of about 13 metres (43 feet), showing that it was built in a series of stepped units out of ashlar-faced rubble, secured with tile courses.

Sewage and drains

By the late first century BC, some of Rome's drains were big enough for inspection boats to sail through. Britain's Roman towns and forts were never equipped with anything so grandiose, but disposing of human waste was still important. At the legionary fortress of York, an impressive system of vaulted stone sewers, 1.5 metres in height, carried sewage away. Fed by smaller side sewers, the main channel was nearly tall enough for a man to walk through and stretches have survived intact.

***

The end of Roman administration in Britain at the beginning of the fifth century did not mean the end of all Roman buildings. In 685 St Cuthbert toured Carlisle's Roman city walls, admiring a working aqueduct and fountain. But Carlisle was exceptional. For the most part, Romano-British buildings fell into ruin. Only in the seventh century did Anglo-Saxon church builders revive stone and brick architecture in Britain, often robbing derelict Roman structures for tile and masonry. The church at Bishop Escomb (Durham) was built of blocks from the nearby fort at Binchester. Brixworth church (Northamptonshire), begun in the late seventh century, made extensive use of Roman brick and tile. At St Albans, the ruins of the Roman town were ransacked for material to use in the great medieval abbey. Dover's lighthouse was modified for Saxon and medieval use as a church belfry. Despite the vigorous programme of Norman castle and cathedral building, beginning in the late eleventh century, architecture in Britain did not compete with the Roman period for quantity and variety until the seventeenth and eighteenth centuries.

9
Further reading

The author's *Buildings of Roman Britain* (1991 and 2001) remains the only full-length popular work on the subject, with a comprehensive bibliography. The other works listed here all have extensive illustrations and/or wide-ranging discussions about general or specific sites. The journal *Britannia*, published by the Society of Roman Studies in London, has an annual compendium of discoveries across Britain (details from the Secretary, Roman Society, Senate House, Malet Street, London WC1E 7HU; website: www.sas.ac.uk/icls/roman/). An invaluable source of up-to-date information about the latest discoveries is the magazine *Current Archaeology*, available by subscription from 9 Nassington Road, London NW3 2TX; website: www.archaeology.co.uk

Bidwell, P., and Holbrook, N. *Hadrian's Wall Bridges*. English Heritage, 1989.
Breeze, D. J. *Roman Forts in Britain.* Shire, 1983; second edition 2002.
Breeze, D.J., and Dobson, B. *Hadrian's Wall.* Penguin, fourth edition, 2000.
Burnham, B.C., and Wacher, J. *The Small Towns of Roman Britain.* Batsford, 1990.
Crow, J. *Housesteads.* Batsford/English Heritage, 1995.
Cunliffe, B. *Fishbourne. A Roman Palace and Its Garden.* Tempus, 1998 (revised reissue of the 1971 edition).
Cunliffe, B. *Roman Bath Discovered.* Tempus, 1999 (revised reissue of the 1984 edition).
de la Bédoyère, G. *Hadrian's Wall. A History and Guide.* Tempus, 1998.
de la Bédoyère, G. *The Golden Age of Roman Britain.* Tempus, 1999. (Villas and mosaics.)
de la Bédoyère, G. *The Buildings of Roman Britain.* Tempus, 2001.
Johnson, A. *Roman Forts.* A. & C. Black, 1983.
Johnson, P. *Romano-British Mosaics.* Shire, 1995 (amended reissue of second edition, 1987).
Johnson, P., and Haynes, I. (editors). *Architecture in Roman Britain.* CBA, 1996.
Johnson, S. *The Roman Forts of the Saxon Shore.* Elek, 1976; second edition, 1979.
Johnston, D. *Discovering Roman Britain.* Shire, third edition, 2002.
Landels, J.G. *Engineering in the Ancient World.* Constable, 2000.
Ling, R. *Romano-British Wall Painting.* Shire, 1985.

Morgan, M.H. *Vitruvius. The Ten Books on Architecture*. Dover, 1960 (and reprints).
Rook, T. *Roman Baths in Britain.* Shire, 1992; reprinted 2002.
Wacher, J. *The Towns of Roman Britain*. Batsford, 1995.
Ward-Perkins, J.B. *Roman Imperial Architecture*. Pelican, 1981.
White, R., and Barker, P. *Wroxeter. Life and Death of a Roman City*. Tempus, 1998.
Wilson, R.J.A. *A Guide to the Roman Remains in Britain*. Constable, 1988 (and reprints).

56. The Multangular Tower at York. Built probably by Constantius I *c*.306–7 as one of a series of prestigious river-front tower embellishments to the legionary and northern provincial government headquarters. The upper part is medieval.

10
Museums and sites

Most Roman buildings in Britain that can be visited today are in the north and the west but there is still plenty to see in the south and the east, and in Wales. The most cost-effective method is to join English Heritage at Customer Services, PO Box 569, Swindon SN2 2YP (telephone: 01793 414910; email: members@english-heritage.org.uk), which will give free access to a full range of Roman buildings.

Bath, Stall Street, Bath, Somerset BA1 1LZ. Telephone: 01225 477774. Website: www.romanbaths.co.uk (Remains of the bathing complex, temple precinct and temple architecture.)

Bignor Roman Villa, Pulborough, West Sussex RH20 1PH. Telephone: 01798 869500. (Villa rooms, a magnificent series of mosaic floors, and site finds.)

Birdoswald Fort, near Gilsland, Cumbria CA8 7DD. Telephone: 01697 747602. Website: www.birdoswaldromanfort.org (Fort platform, defences, gates, granaries and stretch of Hadrian's Wall with milecastle.)

The British Museum, Great Russell Street, London WC1B 3DG. Telephone: 020 7323 8000. Website: www.thebritishmuseum.ac.uk (Mosaics; the Meonstoke façade.)

Castle Museum, Castle Park, Colchester, Essex CO1 1TJ. Telephone: 01206 282939. Website: www.colchestermuseums.org.uk (Remains of the vaults of the temple of Claudius.)

Chesters Roman Fort, Chollerford, Northumberland NE46 4EP. Telephone: 01434 681379. (Fort buildings including bath-house. Bridge abutment nearby to the east – ask for directions at the fort.)

Corbridge Roman Site Museum, Corbridge, Northumberland NE45 5NT. Telephone: 01434 632349. (Military buildings, temples and granaries.)

Corinium Museum, Park Street, Cirencester, Gloucestershire GL7 2BX. Telephone: 01285 655611. Website: www.cotswold.gov.uk (Reconstructed rooms, architectural fragments, directions to city walls and amphitheatre.)

Fishbourne Roman Palace, Salthill Road, Fishbourne, Chichester, West Sussex PO19 3QR. Telephone: 01243 785859. Website: www.sussexpast.co.uk (First-century palace rooms and finds.)

Housesteads Roman Fort, Bardon Mill, Northumberland NE47 6NN. Telephone: 01434 344363. (Fort platform, gates, internal buildings including granaries and latrine.)

Lullingstone Roman Villa, Eynsford, Kent DA4 0JA. Telephone: 01322 863467. (Baths, villa rooms, mosaic floor – all under cover.)

Museum of London, 130 London Wall, London EC2Y 5HN. Telephone: 020 7600 3699. Website: www.museumoflondon.org.uk (Various architectural features.)

Pevensey Castle, Pevensey, East Sussex BN24 5LE. Telephone: 01323 762604. (Saxon Shore fort with gate bastions and medieval castle.)

Portchester Castle, Portchester, Hampshire PO16 9QW. Telephone: 02392 378291. (Saxon Shore fort.)

Richborough Roman Fort, Sandwich, Kent CT13 9JW. Telephone: 01304 612013. (Saxon Shore fort, and triumphal arch foundations.)

Roman Legionary Museum, High Street, Caerleon, Newport NP6 1AE. Telephone: 01633 423134. Website: www.nmgw.ac.uk (Legionary baths, defences and arena.)

Royal Albert Memorial Museum, Queen Street, Exeter, Devon EX4 3RX. Telephone: 01392 665858. Website: www.exeter.gov.uk/tourism/museums/info.html (Legionary baths model, reconstructed lifesize bath apse and washbasin, plus other architectural fragments.)

Segedunum Roman Fort, Buddle Street, Wallsend NE28 6HR. Telephone: 0191 295 5757. Website: www.twmuseums.org.uk/segedunum (Fort platform, museum with reconstructed rooms and replica bath-house.)

Silchester Roman City. The remains of the Roman city walls and the amphitheatre can be visited at any time. They lie close to the village of Silchester near Reading at NGR SU 643624 (OS sheet 175).

South Shields Arbeia Roman Fort, Baring Street, South Shields NE33 2BB. Telephone: 0191 454 4093. (Fort granaries, reconstructed fourth-century house, barrack and gate.)

Verulamium Museum, St Michaels, St Albans, Hertfordshire AL3 4SW. Telephone: 01727 751810. Website: www.stalbansmuseums.org.uk (Fragments from buildings, town house with mosaic, and directions to the Roman theatre nearby.)

Vindolanda Roman Fort Museum, Bardon Mill, Hexham, Northumberland NE47 7JN. Telephone: 01434 344277. Website: www.vindolanda.com (Fort platform and defences, and civilian settlement, as well as reconstructed sections of Hadrian's Wall.)

Welwyn Roman Baths, Welwyn Bypass, Welwyn, Hertfordshire AL6 9NX. Telephone 01707 271362. Website: www.hertsmuseums.org.uk/welwyn-roman-baths (The baths of a third-century villa preserved under the A1(M).)

Wroxeter Roman City, Shrewsbury, Shropshire SY5 6PH. Telephone: 01743 761330. (Site museum adjacent to the exposed remains of the town baths and exercise hall.)

Yorkshire Museum, Museum Gardens, York YO1 7FR. Telephone: 01904 551800. (Inscriptions, architectural features, and city walls in the gardens.)

Index

Page numbers in italic refer to illustrations

PERTH AND KINROSS LIBRARIES